FREE PRESS and FAIR TRIAL

Some Dimensions of the Problem

Free Press
and
Fair Trial

Some Dimensions of the Problem

FRED S. SIEBERT

WALTER WILCOX

GEORGE HOUGH III

Edited by

CHILTON R. BUSH

UNIVERSITY OF GEORGIA PRESS
ATHENS

Copyright © 1970

University of Georgia Press

Library of Congress Catalog Card Number: 70-138674

Printed in the United States

Contents

The Authors

CHILTON R. BUSH, Professor Emeritus of Communication, Stanford University; Director, News Research Center, American Newspaper Publishers Association

GEORGE A. HOUGH III, Associate Professor of Journalism, Michigan State University; former reporter on the *Detroit Free Press* and other newspapers

FRED S. SIEBERT, Research Professor, Michigan State University; Dean Emeritus, College of Communication Arts, Michigan State University; member of the Illinois bar; author of *Freedom of the Press in England* and *Rights and Privileges of the Press*

WALTER WILCOX, Professor of Journalism, and former Chairman, Department of Journalism, University of California (Los Angeles)

Foreword

THE relationship of jury verdicts in felony cases and pretrial publicity is a field of study that has been somewhat neglected by both legal scholars and communication specialists. To partially remedy the insufficiency of objective evidence, the American Newspaper Publishers Association Foundation in November, 1947, commissioned three studies to measure the dimensions of the problem. How important, really, is the problem? Are there a good many or only a few cases in which it is possible for pretrial publicity to influence a jury verdict? Do judges who have tried felony cases believe that the problem is of great importance? Have studies been made that indicate there is a high or a low relationship between the two variables?

A grant was made to Dr. Fred S. Siebert of Michigan State University to interview a national sample of trial judges on the question of miscarriage of justice in their courts as the result of publication of news about crime. Dr. Siebert employed the National Opinion Research Center at the University of Chicago to do the interviewing.

Dr. Siebert included several questions about granting of access by reporters and photographers to judicial proceedings. They are not directly related to the main question he was studying, but the findings are presented here for the purpose of describing the situation (Chapter 4).

Data as to the proportion of felony cases tried by juries and the proportion reported by newspapers have not been available. To provide an analysis of the magnitude of the situation, a grant was made to George Hough III of Michigan State University. He analyzed the disposition in the Detroit Recorder's Court and the reporting in one Detroit newspaper of all felony cases for which warrants of arrest had been issued over a six-month period.

A grant was also made to Dr. Walter Wilcox of the University of California at Los Angeles to search the literature on the subject of jurors and the effect on verdicts of published or broadcast pretrial news. Dr. Wilcox's analysis (*The Press, the Jury, and the Behavioral Sciences*) was published in October, 1968, as Journalism Monograph No. 9 by the Association for Education in Journalism. It is reprinted here by permission of the publishers.

This volume presents the findings from each of the studies. The data will be helpful in determining whether or not further research in this field would be rewarding. The data will also assist those members of the press, bench, and bar who are engaged in developing measures of accommodation between the two basic social values.

Chilton R. Bush

. . . I . . .

Trial Judges' Opinions
on Prejudicial Publicity

Fred S. Siebert

THE purpose of this study, basically, was to learn whether or not judges thought that pretrial publicity had ever resulted in miscarriage of justice in their courts. Such a question could not be asked directly because the prudent and cautious judge would not risk the chance that such an admission would constitute ground for an appeal in some case he had heard; so the judges were asked to evaluate the effectiveness of the several safeguards available to the defendant. They were also asked to state their agreement or disagreement with the statement of an anonymous federal judge that "the ultimate blame for failure of a trial . . . must rest upon the judiciary" (Question 18-B in the appended questionnaire).

As of this time no scientific experimental studies have been conducted to establish the proposition that juries are affected by pretrial or during-trial publicity. Undocumented claims have been made that such publicity has affected or has not affected the outcome of felony trials. Equally undocumented have been the claims that the press has adequately performed its function of serving as a "watch dog" over law enforcement and the judicial process.

From the data presented in this report, it is hoped that some tentative inferences can be made concerning the dimensions of the problem and also concerning the relative effectiveness of some of the existing procedural safeguards.

I would like to acknowledge the valuable assistance of John Kochevar, graduate assistant in Communications at Michigan State University, in preparing the tables and checking the data. Mr. Kochevar, who has the B.S. and M.A. degrees, is a candidate for the Ph.D. degree at Michigan State University.

1

THE DESIGN OF THE STUDY

The method used in this study was to question by personal interview a scientifically determined national sample of all trial judges, both federal and state, who have at one time or another presided at a felony trial. Through the cooperation of Colonel John Carmody, Director of the Section of Judicial Administration of the American Bar Association, the Association's list of trial judges numbering approximately 4,000 was made available and was the basic sampling frame for this study.

The construction of the sample and the interviewing was done by the National Opinion Research Center, University of Chicago, under a grant from the American Newspaper Publishers Association Foundation.

A sampling fraction of .15 was used to yield a sample of 600 judges which was expected to shrink to about 500 because of non-availability or no criminal trial experience. The actual size of the completed sample was 483.

The National Opinion Research Center maintains a national sample of 73 primary sampling areas, selected with probabilities proportionate to population. In the ten largest metropolitan areas, which had initially been selected with certainty, 15 percent of the judges were selected, using a random start and systematic sampling. Within smaller areas that had initially been selected with probabilities of less than one, the sampling fractions were increased so that the overall sampling rate remained .15. Those primary sampling areas with less than 300,000 population were combined into clusters of 300,000, and all judges in the selected clusters were interviewed so that here too the overall sampling fraction of .15 was maintained.

The following data indicate the size of the sample:

Initial sample size	607
Ineligible (no felony trial experience)	85
Net sample size	545
Completed cases	483

The difference between the net sample size and completed cases is due to illness (4), temporarily unavailable (22), refused (25), moved (2), interview too late to be processed (9).

A calculation indicates for most percentages an estimated standard sampling error of .025 or less, taking into account both clustering and finite correction factors. Hence .95 confidence limits would extend from 5 percentage points below to 5 percentage points above the estimated proportion. In short, NORC concludes that "it is highly probable that nearly all estimated proportions are within 5 percentage points of the true value."

In the tables included in this report column percentages total 100 percent of the responses with the exception of rounding errors. The number of judges in each table is 483 except when otherwise indicated.

THE TRIAL JUDGES

As indicated above, 483 judges were interviewed in a national sample. A copy of the questionnaire is in Appendix B of this chapter. Of the sample, 21 (4.3%) trial judges were on the federal bench and 462 (95.6%) presided in state courts. The entire sample was broken down by regions corresponding to the National Reporter System of publishing appellate court decisions. Results for most individual states would have been inconclusive because of the size of the sample. The following is a breakdown of judges by region:

Table 1. Number of Judges Per Region*

Region	Number of judges	Percent
Atlantic	83	17.1
Northeastern	90	18.6
Northwestern	81	16.7
Pacific	117	24.2
Southeastern	22	4.5
Southern	54	11.1
Southwestern	36	7.4

*Lay readers should distinguish the regions of the National Reporter system from those of the United States Census. Appendix A lists the states in each National Reporter region.

Of the 483 trial judges interviewed, 409 had presided at one or more felony cases during the past year (1968). Seventy-three reported they had not tried any felony cases during the past year (one judge did not answer). The experience of these judges in felony trials ranged from 1 to 35 years. The median was 7 years; the average number of years experience was 9.3 years.

NEWSPAPER COVERAGE OF FELONY TRIALS

Each of the judges in the national sample was asked "How many different newspapers cover your court regularly?" The answers are in Table 2.

Table 2. Number of Newspapers Covering Each Court

Number of newspapers	Number of judges	Percent
1	97	20.1
2	155	32.1
3	95	19.7
4	54	11.2
5	33	6.8
6	11	2.3
7 or more	21	4.4
No answer	17	3.5

THE SAFEGUARDS

It has been widely assumed that a number of procedural techniques common in felony trials have at least a tendency either to minimize or eliminate any bias which jurors may acquire from both pre-trial and during the trial published news reports. No scientific evidence has yet been gathered to validate these assumptions as to the effects of such procedural devices as change of venue, use of another venire (list of prospective jurors from another county), *voir dire* (examination of potential jurors), sequestration of the jury during the trial, admonitions from the bench, severance of jointly accused defendants, and granting of continuances to allow the effects of publicity to decline.

Additional *post-trial* safeguards designed to remedy any jury bias which may have occurred include motions for a new trial, appeals to high courts based on jury bias, and the more infrequent use of the writ of habeas corpus to remedy prejudicial verdicts.

An attempt was made in the current study to sample the opinions of trial judges on the effectiveness of these safeguards in eliminating jury bias due to prejudicial news reports.

The answers of the judges to questions on the safeguards described above should also provide some information on frequency of jury bias due to prejudicial news reports.

CHANGE OF VENUE

The most commonly used device for offsetting the effects of pre-trial publicity for felony offences is the motion, usually by defense attorneys, for a change of venue. This is a request presented to the judge to move the trial to another jurisdiction where, it is assumed, the published news reports in newspapers or on radio or television have not had as wide a distribution as they were presumed to have had in the original jurisdiction.

Two hundred and nineteen judges (45.3%) reported that sometime during their tenure as judge they received at least one motion for a change of venue based on publicity. A total of 263 (54.4%) said they had never been asked to rule on a motion for a change of venue because of publicity. Table 3 reports the number of motions received by the 219 judges who had received one or more motions for change of venue.

Table 3. Frequency of Motions for Change of Venue

Number of motions received	Number of judges receiving motions*	Percent
1 to 5	153	70.0
6 to 10	31	14.1
11 to 20	21	9.1
Over 20	7	3.1
No answer	7	3.1
Number	219	

*264 Judges said they had never received a motion for change of venue because of a pretrial and during trial news report.

In response to an inquiry on the number of such motions during the past year (1968), 360 judges (76.8%) reported none, 122 (25.2%) reported one or more such requests in the last year.

The judges were then asked, "In how many cases out of this total would you estimate that you granted the motion for a change of venue?" The answers would indicate that in 20.4 percent of the cases, the motion was granted.

The judges were then asked to follow through and to recall, if possible, whether in the cases where the motion for a change of venue was granted the prejudicial publicity was published on (1) the radio, (2) on television, or (3) in newspapers. The answers are in Table 4. Unfortunately, the results of this question do not indicate the relative prevalence of prejudicial publicity in the three media since there exists a wide difference in the degree to which each covers crime and trial news.

VENIRE FROM ANOTHER JURISDICTION

A procedure somewhat similar to a request for a change of venue is the motion to bypass the venire (list of prospective jurors from the original jurisdiction) and to request the jury be chosen from a venire from another part of the state where it is presumed the possibly prejudicial publicity has not penetrated. It is apparent

Table 4. News Media Mentioned for Prejudicial Publicity in
Motion for Change of Venue*

	TV	Radio	Newspaper
Yes	16.3%	19.8%	41.8%
No	28.5	25.0	2.8
Not applicable	54.6	54.6	54.6
Not answered	0.4	0.4	0.6
N=	483	483	483

*Responses to the question, "Can you recall a motion for a change of venue
which specifically cited the role of television (radio, a newspaper) in reporting
a case?" (Qs. 1-D, 1-E, 1-F).

from the responses of the judges that this device is infrequently
employed to avoid jury bias. Only 58 judges (12%) out of the total
of 483 reported they had ever received such a request while 422
judges indicated that this procedural device had never been used
in their courts. Three judges did not answer the question.

VOIR DIRE

The process of examination of prospective jurors and final selection is designed to eliminate jury bias which may result from several
causes including publicity. Responses to the question "How is the
voir dire examination of prospective jurors usually conducted in your
court?" are shown in Table 5.

Table 5. Persons Conducting *Voir Dire*

	Number of judges	Percent
Judge alone	57	11.8
Attorneys alone	132	27.3
Both judge and attorneys	287	59.3
No answer	7	1.4

The sample of judges was asked: "How often are jurors accepted
who have learned about the case from published news reports but
who say that they can *disregard* what they have learned?" The
answers are reported in Table 6.

Apparently there are considerable differences among states on both
the rules and practice of accepting jurors who have learned about
the case before being called.

In the Pacific region, 16.1 percent of the judges in that area reported they "always" accept such jurors while only 2.5 percent of

Table 6. Frequency of Accepting Jurors Who Say They Have Learned About the Case From Published Reports

	Number of judges	Percent of all judges	Percent applicable
Always or practically always accepted	47	9.7	10.3
Most of the time	134	27.7	29.6
About half the time	49	10.1	10.8
Occasionally	128	26.5	28.3
Never or practically never	94	19.4	20.7
Not applicable	21	4.3	
No answer	10	2.0	

the judges in the Northwest always accept them. In the Atlantic region, 29.6 percent of the judges in those states reported they "never" accept such jurors, while only 5.6 percent of the judges in the Southern region always eliminate such jurors.

An attempt was made to find out how often trial judges sustain a challenge for cause when prospective jurors on *voir dire* admit they have read or heard that the defendant has confessed to the crime. The answers are in Table 7.

Table 7. Frequency of Sustaining Challenge for Cause When Venireman Admits Hearing of Confession

	Number of judges	Percent of all judges	Percent ruling on challenge
Always or practically always	137	28.3	39.4
Most of the time	48	9.9	13.8
About half the time	7	1.4	2.0
Occasionally	30	6.2	8.6
Never or practically never	125	25.8	36.0
No occasion to rule	124	25.6	
No answer	12	1.8	

Here again, state law and court practice vary widely on the question of whether a prospective juror who has read about a confession should be permitted to serve as a juror. More than one-third of the trial judges who have had occasion to rule on such motions practically never sustain a challenge for cause where the prospective juror has read about a confession.

The practice of sustaining challenges to prospective jurors who indicate they have read that the accused has confessed varies in different regions. In the Northwest region 45.7 percent of the judges in that region reported they "always" sustain the challenge in such cases, while only 15.8 percent of the judges in the Pacific region indicated they would "always" sustain challenge for such a cause.

The question of whether a particular venireman (prospective juror) can effectively disregard all prior information which he has received about the case has been debated at length in legal circles. The judges were asked to state their agreement or disagreement with the following quotation: "The mere fact that people are informed cannot be construed to mean that they cannot make a fair and impartial determination of the guilt or innocence of anyone accused of a crime."

More than three-quarters of the judges, (369, 76.3%) indicated agreement with the above statement. Only 87 (18%) disagreed. Seventeen judges either had no opinion or did not answer (5.5%).

A number of judges noted that given the pervasiveness of mass media coverage today, it is practically impossible to obtain a jury of persons who have no knowledge whatsoever about the case before them.

One suggested procedure for detecting bias in a juror in a trial which has been widely publicized is for the prospective juror to be examined privately on his knowledge of the case, away from selected jurors or other prospective jurors. Approval or disapproval of such a procedure is shown in Table 8.

Table 8. Judges' Opinions on Examining Jurors Privately

	Number of judges	Percent
Necessary	162	33.5
Desirable but not necessary	8	1.6
Unnecessary	295	61.0
No opinion	15	3.1
No answer	3	.6

While more than half of the trial judges in the Atlantic region favored examining jurors in private, only 22.6 percent of the judges in the Pacific area favored this procedure.

SEQUESTRATION OF JURY

An attempt was made in the interviews to elicit the judges' opinions on the frequency of sequestering the jury during a widely-reported felony trial as a protection against published news reports of the crime.

Judges were asked to estimate how often in their experience the jury has been isolated. The answers are in Table 9.

Table 9. Frequency of Juror Sequestration

	Number of judges	Percent of all judges	Percent using Procedures
Always or practically always	66	13.6	16.2
Most of the time	38	7.8	9.3
About half the time	8	1.6	1.9
Occasionally	67	13.8	16.5
Never or practically never	178	36.8	43.8
Only in capital crimes	49	10.1	12.0
No occasion to rule	73	15.0	
No answer	4	.8	

Aside from trials for capital offences, the practice of sequestering the jury during widely-publicized felony trials varies widely. In the Southern region, 37 percent of the judges reported "always" while 52.1 percent of the judges in the Pacific region "never" sequester the jury.

THE JUDGE'S ADMONITION

The judges were next asked to comment on the frequency with which they had admonished jurors not to read or listen to reports about the trial or the defendant in widely reported cases when the jury had not been sequestered.

Eighty-one point seven percent (395) of the judges in the sample reported that they "always" or "practically always" admonished jurors not to read or listen to news reports about the trial. Only 3.5 percent (17 judges) reported that they "never" or "practically never" warn jurors against reading or listening about the trial. No attempt was made by the interviewer to determine why these seventeen judges do not admonish juries.

When asked whether they had ever had reason to believe that their admonition had *not* been complied with, 27.9 percent of the judges said "yes," 69.8 percent said "no," and 2.3 percent did not answer.

SEVERANCE AND CONTINUANCE

Two additional devices which are employed to offset possible jury bias due to prejudicial publicity are severance (separate trials for joint defendants) and continuance (postponement of the trial for a "cooling-off" period). A total of 306 judges out of 483 reported that severance had been used in felony trials over which they presided while 166 indicated that a motion for severance based on publicity had never been made in their courts. Eleven judges did not report on this question.

A request for a continuance of a trial to some future date based on what might be considered aroused public reaction is quite frequent. Two hundred and fifty-one judges reported that in one or more trials they had received such a motion based on unfavorable publicity, while 228 judges indicated they had never received such a motion. Four judges did not answer.

RELATIVE EFFECTIVENESS OF SAFEGUARDS

An attempt was made to elicit the judges' opinions on the relative effectiveness of current court procedures designed to protect the defendant against an unfair trial by a biased jury.

More than half of the responding judges (54.4%) indicated they had never been asked to rule on a motion for a change of venue* based on possible prejudicial publicity. The evaluations of the remaining judges are shown in Table 10.

Table 10. Judges' Evaluation of Change of Venue Effectiveness

	Number of judges	Percent	Percent applicable
Highly effective	59	12.2	32.0
Moderately effective	83	17.1	45.1
Ineffective	42	8.6	22.8
Not applicable or no answer	299	61.8	

It would appear that a number of judges concluded that a change of venue was not a complete answer to the situation where a felony defendant has been given a high degree of publicity. The fact that most mass media of communications today tend to saturate an entire state may have influenced this opinion. To move a trial from one county to another within the state may not in many cases avoid the possibility of a biased jury.

Even more rare as a safeguard for the defendant than a change of venue is a motion to use a venire (list of prospective jurors) from another county or jurisdiction. Three judges in the sample did

---

*In New Jersey a special assignment judge rules on such motions.

not answer this question, and 422 (87.3%) reported that they had never received such a motion. Of those judges who had experience with a request for a venire from another county (58), 18 (31.0%) rated it as a "highly effective" device; 25 (43.1%) rated it as "moderately effective"; and 15 (25.8%) indicated that in their opinion it was "ineffective."

A commonly used device for detecting and eliminating jury bias based on prejudicial publicity is the *voir dire* or examination of prospective jurors, usually by attorneys and in some instances with the participation of the judge. Only 38 (7.8%) of the responding judges indicated that this device was *not* used in their courts for the purpose of detecting bias.

The judges' rating of the effectiveness of the *voir dire* is shown in Table 11.

Table 11. Judges' Evaluation of *Voir Dire* Effectiveness

	Number of judges	Percent
Highly effective	214	44.3
Moderately effective	172	35.6
Ineffective	22	4.5
Not used or no answer	75	15.4

Although 188 trial judges reported that they had never ordered a jury *sequestered* in a felony trial, those judges with experience with this device believed that in most cases it was highly effective in reducing any jury bias resulting from adverse publicity preceding the trial. The judges' opinions on the effectiveness of sequestration of the jury during the felony trial are shown in Table 12.

Table 12. Judges' Evaluation of Sequestration Effectiveness

	Number of judges	Percent of all judges	Percent using procedures
Highly effective	157	32.5	60.6
Moderately effective	68	14.0	26.2
Ineffective	34	7.0	13.1
No experience	188	38.9	
No answer	36	7.4	

The most commonly used method for overcoming possible jury bias is the *admonition* or instructions from the bench. These instructions normally include a warning to the jurors not to read or listen to published news reports of the trial and to base their verdict solely on the evidence presented in court.

Only 26 judges (5.3%) indicated they did not use this device to minimize the effects of publicity. The judges' opinions as to the effectiveness of the admonition are reported in Table 13.

Table 13. Judges' Evaluation of Admonition Effectiveness

	Number of judges	Percent of all judges	Percent answering
Highly effective	159	32.9	37.9
Moderately effective	196	40.5	46.8
Ineffective	64	13.2	15.3
Not used	26	5.3	
No answer	38	7.8	

The evidence would seem to indicate that, in the opinion of judges, the effects of news reports published *during the progress of the trial* are at least minimized if not eradicated by instructions from the bench. Obviously the effect of published reports on the jury depends on the persuasive talents of the judge as well as on the receptivity of the individual jurors. Apparently some judges are not sure that their instructions not to read or listen to news reports of the trial are always followed by members of the jury.

As to the effect of admonitions on jurors, the comments of the judges ranged from "A juror's mind can no more be cleansed of information than a bell can be unrung" to the statement, "In the large majority of cases I don't think newspaper stories influence a jury to any material degree."

A not uncommon device for minimizing the effects of pretrial publicity on jurors is a motion for a *continuance* made by attorneys in the case, most commonly by defense attorneys but occasionally by prosecutors. Almost half the responding judges (47.2%) reported that they had never received a motion for a continuance based on possible prejudicial publicity.

The judges' evaluation of the effectiveness of this device in minimizing the effects of publicity is shown in Table 14.

Of those judges in whose court such a motion based on prejudicial publicity has been made, 23.5 percent rated the device as highly effective in minimizing the effects of such publicity, 58.5 percent rated it moderately effective, and 17.9 percent ineffective.

The judicial procedure whereby codefendants can request separate trials (*severance*) is occasionally used to offset unfavorable publicity

Table 14. Judges' Evaluation of Continuance Effectiveness

	Number of judges	Percent of all judges	Percent receiving motion
Highly effective	59	12.2	23.5
Moderately effective	147	30.4	58.5
Ineffective	45	9.3	17.9
Never received such a motion	228	47.2	
No answer	4	0.8	

concerning one or more of the defendants. Table 15 shows that 34.3 percent of the judges interviewed had never been asked to rule on a motion for severance based on published news reports of felonies.

Of the slightly more than 300 judges who had at some time in their careers received a motion for *severance* based on possible prejudicial publicity, only a third believed that this procedure was highly effective in minimizing jury bias, as shown in Table 15.

Table 15. Judges' Evaluation of Severance Effectiveness

	Number of judges	Percent of all judges	Percent receiving motion
Highly effective	99	20.4	32.3
Moderately effective	139	28.7	45.4
Ineffective	68	14.0	22.2
No experience	166	34.3	
No answer	11	2.2	

Table 16 summarizes the perceived effectiveness of procedures used during the trial to protect a defendant from pretrial publicity:

Post-Trial Procedures

At least three procedures are available after the verdict in a felony case to deal with the question of possible jury bias resulting from published news reports circulated either before or during the trial. These are (1) motion for a mistrial or for a new trial, (2) an appeal to a higher court, and (3) a request for a writ of *habeas corpus*. All three of these procedures are normally initiated by attorneys in the case.

An attempt was made to elicit from the 483 judges an opinion as to the effectiveness of the three post-trial procedures in remedying a miscarriage of justice which might have resulted from prejudicial news coverage.

What appears to be an increasingly common practice, where a

Table 16. Summary Table of Judges' Evaluation of Procedures Designed to
Protect Defendants from Pretrial Publicity

	Number of Judges	Highly Effective	Moderately Effective	Ineffective
Sequestration	259	60.6%	26.3%	13.1%
Continuance	251	23.5	58.6	17.9
Severance	306	32.4	45.4	22.2
Change of venue	184	32.1	45.1	22.8
Venire from another county	58	31.0	43.1	25.9
Admonition	419	15.3	46.8	37.9
Voir dire	408	5.4	42.2	52.4

jury verdict unfavorable to the defendant is reached, is a motion
by defense attorneys for a new trial based on jury bias resulting
from what is considered to be unfavorable news reports published
either before or during the trial.

The judges' responses to the question "Have you ever received
a motion for a new trial based on prejudicial news reports?" were as
follows: 122 judges answered "Yes" and 361 answered "No."

The data show that during the past twelve months 36 judges
received one such motion, 13 received two motions for a new trial,
5 received three, and the rest received four or more. Four hundred
and twenty judges or 87 percent of the sample had not received
such a motion during 1968.

In order to further determine the frequency of motions for a
new trial, the judges reported on the number of such motions received
during their careers on the bench, as shown in Table 17.

Table 17. Number and Frequency of Motions for a New Trial

Number of motions	Judges receiving motions	Percent
None	361	74.7
1	41	8.5
2	16	3.3
3	15	3.1
4	5	1.0
5	6	1.2
6-10	20	4.0
11-20	8	1.6
over 20	4	.8
No answer	7	1.4

The judges could recall that in only 35 cases (5.6%) was a
motion for a new trial based on prejudicial publicity granted. Ap-

parently defense attorneys frequently ask for a new trial as a matter of routine, but judges infrequently grant such a motion.

When questioned on the specific medium which carried the publicity, 41 judges reported that the publicity appeared on television; 54 judges reported the material was covered by radio, and 104 reported the publicity appeared in newspapers.

Table 18 indicates the judges' opinions on the effectiveness of a motion for a mistrial or for a new trial.

Table 18. Judges' Evaluation of New Trial or Mistrial Effectiveness

	Number of judges	Percent of all judges	Percent receiving motion
Highly effective	102	21.1	33.1
Moderately effective	119	24.6	38.6
Ineffective	87	18.0	28.2
Never used	170	35.1	
No answer	5	1.0	

Two other procedures have occasionally been used in situations where there may be jury bias due to publicity, an appeal to a higher court and the use of the writ of habeas corpus. No data is available on the frequency of the use of these devices in cases of jury prejudice due to publicity, but 144 judges in the sample reported they had never had a case which was appealed because of prejudicial news reports. Even more rare is the use of the writ of habeas corpus; 154 judges reported that it had never been used in their court for this purpose.

Judges' opinions on the effectiveness of an appeal to a higher court as a remedy for adverse publicity either before or during the trial are reported in Table 19.

Table 19. Judges' Evaluation of Appeal Effectiveness

	Number of judges	Percent of all judges	Percent having experience
Highly effective	106	21.9	32.6
Moderately effective	137	28.3	42.1
Ineffective	82	16.9	25.2
No experience	144	29.8	
No answer	14	2.8	

On the effectiveness of a motion for a writ of habeas corpus after conviction in combating prejudicial news, the judges' opinions are shown in Table 20.

Table 20. Judges' Evaluation of Habeas Corpus Effectiveness

	Number of judges	Percent of all judges	Percent having experience
Highly effective	79	16.3	13.8
Moderately effective	113	23.3	40.2
Ineffective	129	26.7	45.9
No experience	154	31.8	
No answer	8	1.6	

Table 21 shows the relative perceived effectiveness of post-trial procedures designed to protect a defendant from news reports arising during the course of the trial.

Table 21. Summary Table of Judges' Evaluations of Procedures Designed to Protect Defendants from Prejudicial Publicity During a Trial

	Number of Judges	Highly Effective	Moderately Effective	Ineffective	Total
Appeal	325	32.6%	42.2%	25.2%	100%
Motion for mistrial or retrial	308	33.1	38.6	28.3	100
Habeas corpus after conviction	321	24.6	35.2	40.2	100

INFORMATION THAT MAY CONTRIBUTE TO JURY BIAS

Although it is practically impossible to classify or identify the various categories of information which reach jurors or prospective jurors through the mass media of communication, several specific types of information have been isolated as possibly contributing to jury bias in felony cases. These types include (1) the prior criminal record of the defendant, (2) confessions, (3) the results of tests or examinations of the defendant, and (4) arguments before the court on the admissibility of evidence.

Ordinarily in a felony trial, the prior criminal record of the defendant is not admissible as evidence in the instant case. The fact that a defendant has a criminal record is not considered as evidence that he committed this particular crime. Although this information is not admissible at the trial, it is frequently carried by the mass media, particularly in well-publicized cases. The information on the prior criminal record of the defendant is generally available to the mass media either from their own files or from court records or from attorneys or police. No conclusive experimental studies have been made on the possible effect of this information on jury verdicts.

PRIOR CRIMINAL RECORD

The judges' opinions on the appropriateness of publishing the prior criminal record of an accused defendant in a felony case are given in Table 22.

Table 22. Judges' Evaluation of Publication of Criminal Record

	Number of judges	Percent
Generally inappropriate to publish	417	86.3
Appropriate in some circumstances	29	6.0
Generally appropriate	32	6.6
No opinion	5	1.0

The judges' gratuitious comments on the "prior criminal record" issue range from "Once a person has been arrested and charged the public has a right to know the background of that individual" to "They shouldn't be publishing anything about his previous record."

At the time the interviews with the judges were taking place, the mass media were carrying reports about the alleged assassin of the Rev. Martin Luther King. Most of these reports contained the prior criminal record of the accused. The sample was asked to comment on the publicity and their answers are reported in Table 23.

Table 23. Judges' Evaluation of the Publication of the Criminal Record of Martin Luther King's Alleged Assassin

	Number of judges	Percent
Publicity was inappropriate	296	61.2
Appropriate	153	31.6
Don't know or no answer	34	6.9

CONFESSIONS

Legal circles have been concerned for some time over the possible effects on jurors of the publication in the mass media of the contents of "confessions." These so-called confessions are sometimes released to the press by law-enforcement officers, by attorneys, or by the defendant himself. The admissibility of these statements as evidence in the trial are almost always questioned by defense attorneys and under recent decisions of the United States Supreme Court their acceptance by the judge as evidence has become more infrequent.

Some newspapers in their pre-trial reporting of the felony have tended to avoid the use of the word "confession" and in its place have reported that the defendant made a "statement" and in many cases have published the contents of this statement.

The judges were asked to give their opinions on the appropriateness of releasing the contents of a confession to the press in advance of the trial. Their answers are in Table 24.

Table 24. Judges' Evaluation of the Release of a Confession

	Number of judges	Percent
Inappropriate to release confessions	466	96.4
Appropriate in some circumstances	9	1.8
Generally appropriate	5	1.0
No opinion or no answer	3	.6

Tests

A third category of information frequently published by the mass media in felony cases is the results of tests or examinations (so-called truth-serum tests, ballistics tests, etc.) or the defendant's refusal to submit to such tests.

The results of these tests or the information that the accused has refused to submit to these tests has in the past been at least occasionally released to the press by law-enforcement officials as well as by both prosecuting and defense attorneys. Again no conclusive experimental study has ever been made of the possible effects of this information on the jury or on prospective jurors.

The judges' opinions of the appropriateness of the release this type of information follows are shown in Table 25.

Table 25. Judges' Evaluation of Releasing the Results of Certain Tests

	Number of judges	Percent
Generally inappropriate to release this information	453	93.7
Appropriate only in some circumstances	21	4.3
Generally appropriate	7	1.4
No opinion or no answer	2	.4

Admissibility of Evidence

Although the above categories of information generally apply to *pre-trial* publicity, the fourth category consists of information from the trial itself. An attempt was made in the interviews with the judges to obtain information on court practices where questions are raised concerning the admissibility of a particular piece of evidence. Normally such arguments are made before the judge *without* the presence of the jury. However, it is not uncommon for both the evidence and the arguments concerning its admissibility to find their way into the mass media and by that route sometimes reach the members of the jury. Whether a juror who receives this information from sources outside the courtroom is thereby biased in his opinion on the guilt or innocence of the defendant has never been determined.

Judges were first asked a general question concerning the presence of reporters during argument on the admissibility of evidence. Their answers are shown in Table 26. Apparently almost three-quarters of the judges permit reporters to listen to arguments about the admissibility of evidence where this argument does not take place in the presence of the jury.

Table 26. Presence of Reporters During Arguments Concerning Admissibility of Evidence

	Number of judges	Percent
Reporters present	353	73.0
Reporters not present	123	25.4
No answer	7	1.4

The judges were then asked whether they admonished the reporters not to publish anything about this segment of the judicial proceeding. Only 124 (25.6%) judges reported that they periodically issued such a warning, and 224 (46.3%) indicated they never give any instructions to the reporters concerning the publication of information on the admissibility of evidence. Five judges did not answer.

The judges who normally caution the reporters in these situations were then asked whether the reporters tended to follow their instructions not to publish this information. Only 14 (11.2%) judges could recall any instance in which the reporters disregarded their instructions.

A specific question was asked to determine the exact procedure the court used during arguments on the admissibility of evidence. These answers can be found in Table 27. Judicial practice apparently varies widely in different jurisdictions. Also the practice seems to vary due to special circumstances in individual cases before the court.

Table 27. Procedure for Hearing Arguments About the Admission of Evidence

	Number of judges	Percent
Arguments heard in court with reporters present	248	51.3
Arguments heard only in chambers	123	25.5
Arguments heard in sidebar conferences	31	6.4
Arguments heard in court without reporters present	10	2.1
Practice varies	68	14.1
No answer	3	.6

From Table 27 we see that reporters are excluded by only 2 percent of the judges. This seems to contradict evidence presented in Table 26 where almost 25 percent of the judges said reporters were not present during argument on the admissibility of evidence. Such a discrepancy is probably the result of the general nature of the question on presence of reporters. Some of the judges apparently responded to this question by noting that reporters were seldom present. The more specific question on procedure reported in Table 27 reveals that while reporters may not be "present" in 25 percent of the courts, they are only specifically excluded during arguments by 2 percent of the judges.

The judges were also asked to respond to the following statement: "The ultimate blame for failure of a fair trial must . . . rest upon the judiciary. Show me an unfair trial that goes uncorrected and I will show you a judge who has failed in his duty."

Only 15 judges in the sample failed to answer, while 281 (58.1%) agreed and 187 judges (38.7%) disagreed with the statement. Coincidentally the trial judge who had made the above statement turned up as a member of the sample.

Among the comments of respondents on the statement were the following:

"The statement really points the finger at the Supreme Court ultimately and that is right."

"It [the statement] might be true in some cases but not generally. The press is often to blame."

"The greatest responsibility rests with the judiciary but disagree with the full statement."

"I don't agree. There are things which happen which if not called to the attention of the court by proper motion, the court has no power to correct."

"Absolutely. The judge has sufficient power in this matter."

"Court can't know what goes on in a jury. They can be prejudiced or biased—who knows?"

"I would only agree if court could control press media."

"The vigorous judge who takes initiative can control publicity."
"A hazy statement."

"Regardless of what precaution a judge may exercise in impanelling a jury, we must be practical in recognizing that if a trial or pre-trial is not reported objectively, it only stands to reason that it is going to be most difficult to seat an entirely impartial jury."

"Take the Sirhan case in California—who knows what judge will try Sirhan. How can they expect a judge to ban the pre-trial behavior of the press or TV?"

PRESS-BAR "CODES"

The free press-fair trial problem has generated a number of plans and suggestions for facilitating voluntary cooperation between the news media on the one hand and the law enforcement officers, prosecutors, attorneys, and judges on the other. At this writing, the press and bar associations and, in some instances, the bench in two-thirds of the states had either adopted a statement of principles or were negotiating one. In several of the states the principles are spelled out with specific guidelines.

In February, 1964, "The Bench-Bar-Press Committee for the State of Washington" was established. The chief justice of the Supreme Court appointed committee members pursuant to a resolution of the State Judicial Council. This Committee has not only adopted a set of principles and voluntary guidelines, but has sponsored workshops in various cities for the education of judges, lawyers, law enforcement officers, and newsmen. The panel which conducts the workshops is composed of the chief justice of the Supreme Court, a lawyer, and a newsman. They explain the guidelines and answer questions. The rationale of this Committee is that the problem can be solved by education. In some other states, joint committees are planning workshops and seminars for the same purpose.

In the present study, the judges were asked whether a press-bar code had been adopted in their jurisdiction. Only 72 (14.9%) of the judges reported that a code was in operation in their communities. In a large majority of the jurisdictions where the judges were questioned, 395 judges (81.7%) reported no code in operation. Sixteen judges either did not know or did not answer.

Of those communities in which a code was in operation, 63 judges (87.5%) indicated that the performance under the code was "good"; 4 said it was "fair"; 2 said it was "poor"; and 3 had no opinion.

In a third question on this subject, the judges were asked whether they favored or opposed a press-bar code for their jurisdiction. More than 50 percent of the judges favored such a code (242), 94 (19.4%) did not feel that a code was the answer; 52 (10.7%) said they didn't know, and 95 (19.6%) did not answer.

The ABA Recommendations

Just prior to the interviews with the judges, the House of Delegates of the American Bar Association adopted the recommendations submitted to it by the Advisory Committee on Fair Trial and Free Press, under the chairmanship of Justice Paul C. Reardon.

Three hundred and thirty-one judges (68.5%) indicated that they were familiar with the recommendations of the Reardon Report; 151 (31.2%) said they were not familiar with the recommendations, and one judge did not answer. Judges in the Pacific region were most familiar with the recommendations (76.7%) while judges in the Southern region were the least familiar (53.7%).

Summary

Three-fourths of the judges reported that they had received from one to five motions for a change of venue based on advance news coverage.

Of the 406 judges who had an opportunity to rule on sequestration of jurors in felony cases, close to one-half (43.8 percent) said they "practically never" sequestered jurors.

The "most highly or moderately" effective safeguards, according to the responding judges, were the judges' admonition to the jury, sequestering the jury, continuance or postponement, and the *voir dire* examination of jurors.

On the effectiveness of post-trial procedures, the judges reported the "most highly or moderate" effective safeguards for protecting a defendant from unfavorable publicity during a trial were an appeal to a higher court and a motion for a new trial.

The judges were generally agreed that in most cases it was inappropriate to publish the prior criminal record of the defendant in a felony trial. An overwhelming majority of the judges considered it inappropriate to release for publication the contents of a "confession" before it had been accepted as evidence in the trial. Almost the same number objected to the publication of the results of tests or examinations prior to the acceptance of these results in court.

The interviews with the judges also show a wide variety of procedures for hearing arguments on the admissibility of evidence.

Only a small number of judges (14.9%) reported a press-bar code in operation in their communities. However, more than 50 percent of the judges favored such a code.

Appendix A

Regions as Organized under the National Reporter System

Atlantic: Connecticut, Delaware, District of Columbia, Maine, Maryland, New Hampshire, New Jersey, Pennsylvania, Rhode Island, Vermont.

Northeastern: Massachusetts, Ohio, Illinois, Indiana, New York.

Northwestern: Iowa, Michigan, Minnesota, Nebraska, North Dakota, South Dakota, Wisconsin.

Pacific: Arizona, California, Colorado, Idaho, Kansas, Montana, Nevada, New Mexico, Oklahoma, Oregon, Washington, Wyoming.

Southeastern: Georgia, North Carolina, South Carolina, Virginia, West Virginia.

Southern: Alabama, Florida, Louisiana, Mississippi.

Southwestern: Arkansas, Missouri, Kentucky, Tennessee, Texas.

Appendix B

National Opinion Research Center
University of Chicago

Confidential
NORC 4051
June, 1968

```
TIME
BEGAN: _____
```

INTRODUCTION

I'm _____ from the National Opinion Research Center at the

University of Chicago.

We're conducting a national survey to get accurate information about trial judges'
experiences with and opinions about pre-trial and during-trial news reports.

We will be interviewing some 500 judges all over the United States, and your name
has fallen into our sample.

Let me assure you that all of your remarks will be treated as confidential, and
that only the statistical results of the study will be made public.

SCREENING QUESTIONS

A. First, during the past year did you try any felony cases in a court of
original jurisdiction?

                              Yes . . (ASK B) . . . 1   10/y

                              No . . (ASK C) . . . 2

B. IF YES: For how many years altogether have you tried felony cases in a
court of original jurisdiction?

            NUMBER OF YEARS: _____ (GO TO Q. 1)   11-12/yy

C. IF NO: Have you ever tried felony cases in a court of original
jurisdiction?

                              Yes . . . . . (ASK D & E) . . . 1   13/y

                              No . .(TERMINATE INTERVIEW). . 2

IF YES TO C:

D. In what year did you last try a felony case?

                                        YEAR: _____   14-15/yy

E. For how many years altogether did you try felony cases in a court
of original jurisdiction?

            NUMBER OF YEARS: _____ (GO TO Q. 1)   16-17/yy

1. The first series of questions has to do with actual experiences and
    practices in your own court.

    First, in your experience as a judge in felony trials, have you ever received
    a motion for a <u>change of venue</u> because of pre-trial and during-trial news
    report?

                                        Yes . . (ASK A-F) . 1   18/y

                                        No   (GO TO Q. 2)   2

    IF YES:

    A. In how many felony trials have you received such a motion or motions
        during the past twelve months?

                          NUMBER: _____   19-20/yy

                          00   NOT APPLICABLE: Did not hear felony
                               cases during the past 12 months

    B. In about how many felony trials would you say you have <u>ever</u> received
        such motions?

                          NUMBER: _____   21-22/yy

    C. In how many cases out of this total would you estimate that you granted
        the motion?

                          NUMBER: _____   23-24/yy

    D. Can you recall a motion for a <u>change of venue</u> which specifically cited
        the role of <u>television</u> in reporting a case?

                                        Yes 1   25/y

                                        No 2

    E. Can you recall any that specifically cited the reporting of a case on
        <u>radio</u>?

                                        Yes 3   26/y

                                        No 4

    F. Can you recall any that specifically cited <u>newspaper</u> reporting of a
        case?

                                        Yes 5   27/y

                                        No 6

2. Have you ever received a motion for a <u>new trial</u> because of news reports
    from the mass media?

                                          Yes . .(ASK A-F). . . 7   28/y

                                          No . (GO TO Q. 3). . 8

    IF YES:

    A. In how many felony trials have you received such a motion or motions
        during the past twelve months?

                          NUMBER: _____   29-30/yy

                          00 NOT APPLICABLE: Did not hear felony
                                 cases during the past 12 months

    B. In about how many felony trials would you say you have ever received
        such motions?
                          NUMBER: _____   31-32/yy

    C. In how many cases out of this total would you estimate that you granted
        the motion?
                          NUMBER: _____   33-34/yy

    D. Can you recall a motion for a <u>new trial</u> which specifically cited the
        role of television in reporting the case?

                                          Yes   1   35/y

                                          No 2

    E. Can you recall any that specifically cited the reporting of a case
        on radio?
                                          Yes 3   36/y

                                          No 4

    F. Can you recall any that specifically cited newspaper reporting of a
        case?
                                          Yes 5   37/y

                                          No 6

3. How is the <u>voir dire</u> examination of prospective jurors usually conducted
    in your court--by the judge alone, by the attorneys, or by the judge <u>and</u>
    the attorneys?

                          Judge alone 1   38/y

                          Attorneys 2

                          Judge and attorneys . . . 3

-4-   DECK 1

4. HAND RESPONDENT CARD A.

A. In your court how often are jurors <u>accepted</u> who have learned about the
    case but who say they can <u>disregard</u> what they have learned--would you say
    always, most of the time, about half the time, occasionally, or never?

                    Always or practically always 1   39/y
                    Most of the time 2
                    About half the time 3
                    Occasionally 4
                    Never or practically never 5
                    Not applicable, don't hear felony cases . . 6

B. How often do you <u>sustain</u> a challenge for cause when prospective jurors
    on <u>voir dire</u> admit they have read that the defendant has <u>confessed</u> to
    the crime--would you say always, most of the time, about half the time,
    occasionally, or never?

                    Always or practically always 1   40/y
                    Most of the time . . . . ∶ 2
                    About half the time 3
                    Occasionally 4
                    Never or practically never 5
                    Not applicable, don't hear felony cases . . 6

C. In <u>widely reported</u> cases, how often is the jury sequestered--would you
    say always, most of the time, about half the time, occasionally, or
    never?

                    Always or practically always 1   41/y
                    Most of the time 2
                    About half the time 3
                    Occasionally 4
                    Never or practically never 5
                    Not applicable, don't hear felony cases . . 6
                    Not applicable, occasion never arises . . . 7

D. In widely reported cases where the jury has <u>not</u> been sequestered, how
    frequently do you admonish the jurors not to read or listen to news
    reports about the trial--would you say always, most of the time, about
    half the time, occasionally, or never?

                    Always or practically always . (ASK E) . . 1   42/y
                    Most of the time . . . . (ASK E) . . 2
                    About half the time . . . . . . (ASK E) . . 3
                    Occasionally . . . . (ASK E) . . 4
                    Never or practically never. 5
                    Not applicable, don't hear felony cases . . 6
                    Not applicable, occasion never arises . . . 7

E. IF AT ALL: In a situation of this type have you ever had reason
                 to believe that your admonition was not complied with?

                                        Yes 8   43/y
                                        No   9

5. When it is necessary to hear argument about the admissibility of evidence outside the presence of the jury, do you ever hear the argument with news reporters present?

                                         Yes . . . (ASK A) 3 44/y

                                         No, never. (GO TO Q. 6). . 4

    A. IF YES: In these situations do you ever direct the news reporters not to publish what they hear?

                                         Yes . . (ASK B) . . . 5 45/y

                                         No. . . (GO TO Q.6) . 6

      B. IF YES: Can you recall any instance where news reporters did not comply with your instructions?

                                         Yes 7 46/y

                                         No. 8

---

6. What is your usual practice when hearing such argument--do you hear it in chambers, at a side-bar conference, in open court after excluding news reporters, (in open court with reporters present), or just what?

                              In chambers 1 47/y

                              Side-bar conference 2

                              In court, reporters excluded. . . . 3

                              In court, reporters not excluded. . 4

                              Other (SPECIFY) 5

7. HAND RESPONDENT CARD B. Next, I'm going to read a list of possible safe-
    guards designed to protect a defendant from pre-trial news reports.

    I'd like you to rate each of these procedures according to how effective they
    have proven to be when used in cases tried in your court. If any have never
    been used in your court, please let me know.

		Effectiveness			
Prodecures		Highly Effective	Moderately Effective	Ineffec-tive	Not applicable; has not been used in my court
A.	The first is change of venue. How effective a safeguard against pre-trial publicity have you found this to be? (...Would you say highly effective, moderately effective, or ineffective?)	1	2	3	4	48/y
B.	How about voir dire? How effec-tive a safeguard have you found this to be?	5	6	7	8	49/y
C.	What about a venire from another county? How effective has this proven to be in your experience?	1	2	3	4	50/y
D.	How about continuance to allow time for any presumed prejudice to subside? (How effective has this been?)	5	6	7	8	51/y
E.	What about severance with respect to one or more jointly-accused defendants? (How effective have you found this to be?)	1	2	3	4	52/y
F.	What about sequestration cf the jury? (How effective has this proven to be in your court?)	5	6	7	8	53/y
G.	What about admonition not to read newspapers, listen to radio or watch television during the trial? (How effective would you say this has been in your experience?)	1	2	3	4	54/y

8.   USE CARD B.   I'd also like to ask about procedures designed to protect a
     defendant from news reports arising during the course of a trial.

Procedures	Effectiveness			
	Highly Effective	Moderately Effective	Ineffective	Not applicable; has not been used in my court
A. Based on your own experience, how effective would you rate the motion for mistrial or retrial--as a highly effective, moderately effective or ineffective safeguard against publicity arising during a trial?	5	6	7	8
B. How effective would you rate the appeal in this regard? (...As highly effective, moderately effective or ineffective?)	1	2	3	4
C. And how effective a safeguard would you rate habeas corpus after conviction? (...As highly effective, moderately effective or ineffective?)	5	6	7	8

55/y (row A), 56/y (row B), 57/y (row C)

9.   It has been suggested that when a crime is widely publicized, each prospective
     juror should be examined privately on his knowledge of the case--that is, away
     from other selected jurors or prospective jurors.

     In your opinion is such a practice necessary or unnecessary in widely publicized
     cases?

                                        Necessary 1   58/y
                                        Unnecessary . . . 2
                                        No opinion 3

-8-   DECK 1

The next few questions have to do with the access of news media personnel to
the courts.

10. A.   First, news reporters. Do news reporters have access to preliminary
         hearings in felony cases under your jurisdiction?

                                        Yes 4   59/y

                                        No   5

                                        Not applicable; no
                                          preliminary hearings . 6

    B.   Do you think they should have access to preliminary hearings in felony
         cases?

                                        Yes 7   60/y

                                        No   8

---

11. A.   Next, news photographers. Are news photographers permitted access to
         the courtroom during criminal proceedings under your jurisdiction?

                         Yes . . . . . (GO TO C)   1   61/y

                         No   . . . .(ASK B) 2

                         Not applicable; don't hear criminal
                           proceedings . . . (SKIP TO Q. 13) . . . 3

    B.   IF NO: Do they have access to court buildings and grounds under your
                 jurisdiction?

                                        Yes 4   62/y

                                        No 5

    C.   ASK EVERYONE: Do you think news photographers should have access to
                        the courtroom during criminal proceedings?

                         Yes .   (GO TO E) . . 6   63/y

                         No .   (ASK D) . . . 7

    D.   IF NO TO C: Do you think they should have access to court buildings
                      and grounds?

                                        Yes 8   64/y

                                        No 9

    E.   ASK EVERYONE: Do you permit sketching in your courtroom during
                        criminal proceedings?

                                        Yes 1   65/y

                                        No 2

12. A. Finally, newsreel and television cameramen. Do cameramen have access to your courtroom during criminal proceedings?

Yes 3   66/y

No 4

B. Do they have access to court buildings and grounds under your jurisdiction?

Yes 6   67/y

No 7

C. Do you think newsreel and television cameramen should have access to a courtroom?

Yes 8   68/y

No 9

D. Do you think they should have access to court buildings and grounds?

Yes 1   69/y

No 2

---

13. In your opinion how appropriate or inappropriate is it to release the content of a confession to the press in advance of a trial--would you say generally appropriate, appropriate but only in some circumstances, or generally inappropriate?

BEGIN
DECK 2

Generally appropriate 3   10/y
Appropriate but only in some
    circumstances . . (ASK A). 4
Generally inappropriate 5
No opinion. 6

A. IF APPROPRIATE BUT ONLY IN SOME CIRCUMSTANCES: In what circumstances? (Any other?)

11/y

12/y

13/y

14/y

15/y

-10- DECK 2

14. In your opinion, how appropriate is it for the news media to publish the prior criminal record of a defendant charged with a crime--would you say generally appropriate, appropriate but only in some circumstances, or generally inappropriate?

Generally appropriate . . . 1 16/y

Appropriate but only in
  some circumstances (ASK A) 2

Generally inappropriate. . . 3

No opinion 4

  A. IF APPROPRIATE BUT ONLY IN SOME CIRCUMSTANCES: In what circumstances?
                                        (Any other?)

17/y

18/y

19/y

20/y

21/y

15. How appropriate do you feel it is to release information to the news media regarding the results of tests or examinations, or of a defendant's refusal or failure to submit to a test or examination--would you say generally appropriate, appropriate but only in some circumstances, or generally inappropriate?

Generally appropriate. . . . 1 22/y

Appropriate but only in
  some circumstances (ASK A) 2

Generally inappropriate . . 3

No opinion 4

  A. IF APPROPRIATE BUT ONLY IN SOME CIRCUMSTANCES: In what circumstances?
                                        (Any other?)

23/y

24/y

25/y

26/y

27/y

16. Does this community operate under a press-bar code of practices governing the coverage of felony trials?

                                              Yes. . (ASK A) . 1   28/y

                                              No . . (ASK C) . 2

    A. IF YES: Would you say that performance under the code has been good, fair, or poor?

                                              Good . (GO TO Q. 17) . 3   29/y

                                              Fair . . . (ASK B) . 4

                                              Poor . . . (ASK B) . 5

                                              No opinion 6

        B. IF FAIR OR POOR: In what ways has the performance been less than good?

                                                                    30/y

                                                                    31/y

                                                                    32/y

                                                                    33/y

                                                                    34/y

    C. IF NO: Would you favor or oppose such a press-bar code in this community?

                                              Favor 1   35/y

                                              Oppose . . . 2

                                              Don't know. . 3

---

17. How many different newspapers regularly cover your court?

                                  NUMBER: _____   36-37/yy

18. HAND RESPONDENT CARD C. I'd like to get your reactions to some statements
     made recently by other judges. Would you agree or disagree with...

		Agree	Disagree	
A.	Statement I. "The mere fact that people are informed cannot be construed to mean that they cannot make a fair and impartial determination of the guilt or innocence of anyone accused of a crime."	1	2	38/y
B.	Statement II. "The ultimate blame for failure of a fair trial must...rest upon the judiciary. Show me an unfair trial that goes uncorrected and I will show you a judge who has failed in his duty."	3	4	39/y

19. The criminal record of the alleged assassin of Martin Luther King has been
     widely publicized. In this particular case, would you say that such publicity
     is appropriate or inappropriate?

                                        Appropriate . . . 5   40/y
                                        Inappropriate . . 6
                                        Don't know . . . 7

20. Are you familiar with the recommendations of the Reardon Report?

                                        Yes 1   41/y
                                        No 2

Thank you, and is there anything else you would like to say about these matters?

TIME	AM
ENDED :———————PM

NAME OF JUDGE: _____

INTERVIEWER SIGNATURE: _____

... II ...

Felonies, Jury Trial, and News Reports

GEORGE A. HOUGH III

THE main objective of this study was to analyze the disposition in one criminal court and the reporting in one newspaper of all felony cases for which warrants of arrest had been issued over a six-months period.

Detroit was selected as the city for investigation primarily because of its accessibility to the researcher and because both of its daily newspapers were readily available on microfilm.

Detroit is the hub of a sprawling metropolitan complex which spreads over Wayne county and into Macomb and Oakland counties. Population of Detroit is 1,649,000 and of the metropolitan area is 4,183,000.[1] Detroit has its own municipal court, the Recorder's Court. This court has original and exclusive jurisdiction in all criminal matters within the city and has jurisdiction in city condemnation cases. The Recorder's Court has a separate and autonomous traffic and ordinance division. There are other courts in Detroit: the Federal District Court, Wayne County Circuit Court, a Court of Common Pleas, and a state Court of Appeals. Within the city and metropolitan area, there are 145 different courts ranging upward from justice courts to the Circuit Court Bench and Appeals Court.[2]

1. *Newspaper Rates and Data*, Vol. 51, No. 1, Jan. 12, 1969. Skokie, Ill: Standard Rate and Data Service, Inc.

2. Data on the Detroit and Detroit metropolitan courts can be found in Virtue, Maxine Boord, *A Survey of Metropolitan Courts: Detroit Area*, Ann Arbor, University of Michigan Law School, 1950, pp. 3-55 and passim. Some changes have taken place in the structure of Michigan courts since this study was completed and further changes are now being planned by the courts and state legislature.

Detroit has two daily newspapers, the morning *Free Press* and the evening *News*. The *Free Press* is published seven days a week and has a weekday circulation of 600,803 and a Sunday circulation of 644,524.[3] The Detroit *News* has a weekday evening circulation of 702,591 and a Sunday circulation of 933,929.[4]

Other than the *Free Press* and *News* in the metropolitan area, there are 36 weekly newspapers in Wayne county, two dailies and 17 weeklies in Oakland county, and two dailies and six weeklies in Macomb county, a grand total of six dailies and 59 weeklies for the three-county metropolitan area.[5]

Every issue of the Detroit *Free Press* was searched during the period November 1, 1966 through April 30, 1967. Every news story concerned with a crime or criminal trial, regardless of the place where the crime was committed or the trial taking place, was tabulated. Civil matters and misdemeanors were not included. The news story about crime in general—for example, interpretative stories about organized crime, crime in the streets, the problem of the battered child—were not included. In other words, every story tabulated was a story about a specific crime or about a specific person accused of a crime. The tabulation was broken down, as Table 1 shows, to indicate the place in which the crime was committed, and an effort was made to predict what court would ultimately try the case.

The data indicates that approximately two-thirds of all the news stories about crimes and criminal trials were concerned with events occurring outside the city limits of Detroit. For example, in November 1966, the *Free Press* published 166 news stories about crimes or criminal trials. Only 56 of these were crimes or trials in which the crime occurred or the trial was held in the city of Detroit. Of the 79 Detroit or metropolitan Detroit cases, 53 were considered to be Recorder's Court cases, three would belong in other Detroit courts and 21 in various other courts in the metropolitan area.

Table 2 tabulates the handling of felony cases in Recorder's Court during the period under study. In this table, the news stories reporting crimes or criminal trials identified as Recorder's Court cases are compared with the volume of cases handled by the Court in each of the six months under study. In November 1966, the *Free Press* carried 53 news stories concerning Recorder's Court cases.

---

3. *Newspaper Rates and Data*, Jan. 12, 1969.
4. *Ibid.*
5. Michigan Press Association, *Michigan Newspaper Directory and Rate Book*, East Lansing, 1969.

Table 1. Number of News Stories, Place in Which Crime was Committed, and Jurisdiction in Which Defendant Should Appear

Month	Number of News Stories	Place of Crime				Jurisdiction - Detroit Area			
		Outside Michigan	Michigan (Outside Greater Det.)	Greater Detroit	Detroit	Number of News Stories	Recorder's Court	Other Detroit	Greater Detroit
November 1966	166	76	11	23	56	79	53	5	21
December 1966	159	74	14	16	55	71	50	4	17
January 1967	158	60	10	34	54	88	52	5	31
February 1967	120	35	12	18	55	73	52	3	18
March 1967	212	73	11	52	76	128	70	6	52
April 1967	173	81	17	30	45	75	42	4	29
Totals	988	399	75	173	341	514	319	27	168
Per cent	100.0	40.4	7.6	17.5	34.5	52.0	32.3	2.7	17.0

Table 2. Felony Cases in Recorder's Court, Nov. 1, 1966-April 30, 1967

	No. of News Stories	Warrants Issued	Defendants Arraigned	Examinations Actually Held	Trials Held
November 1966	53	704	701	177	29
December 1966	50	708	678	257	40
January 1967	52	792	762	299	55
February 1967	52	704	683	392	65
March 1967	70	794	745	330	102
April 1967	42	748	693	231	89
Total	319	4,450	4,262	1,686	380

Source: Recorder's Court Clerk, Annual Reports, 1966, 1967, and statistics compiled for annual reports.

During that month, 704 felony warrants were issued by the Recorder's Court, 701 defendants were arraigned, 177 examinations held, but only 29 trials were held.

Because of the usual lag between arrest and trial, the trials held in November were not necessarily the trials of persons arrested and arraigned in that month. The ratio of warrants issued to trials held, however, indicates that no more than one out of eight warrants results in a trial, and usually the number of trials is less.

Table 3 indicates another interesting fact about newspaper stories about crime and criminal matters. The data suggests that nearly 60 per cent of news stories are about crimes in the investigatory stages, at the time of the commission of the crime, while it is under investigation, and at the time of arrest of suspects. A considerable number of news stories are about crimes in which the offender is unidentified. Fewer stories are published at time of arraignment and fewer at time of trial.

The figures in Table 3 are a little misleading since they are not correlated with the place where the crime was committed or where the trial is held. During the period under study the total for news stories about trials was swelled considerably by the numerous stories published about the second murder trial of Sam Shepard in Cleveland; the legal entanglements of James Hoffa—all post-trial stories, actually—and related to trials held in Federal courts in Tennessee; the two murder trials of Dr. Carl Coppolino, one in New Jersey and one in Florida; and the murder trial of Richard Speck in Illinois. Coverage of these trials was extensive in terms of space, the number of stories carried and the placement of the stories. Local trials were not given similar treatment.

Table 4 adds an interesting dimension to the study, for it suggests that if there are few news stories about crimes, criminal court

Table 3. Nature of All Cases Reported by Detroit *Free Press*, November 1, 1966–April 30, 1967

Month	Investigation		Arraigned	Pre-trial	Other Hearings	Trials	Total
	Suspects not Known	Suspects Named					
November 1966	47	58	14	16	4	27	166
December 1966	46	42	17	17	9	28	159
January 1967	41	38	21	14	17	27	158
February 1967	45	32	13	13	12	5	120
March 1967	85	58	16	7	28	18	212
April 1967	47	47	19	5	18	37	173
Total	311	275	100	72	88	142	988
Per cent	31.5	27.8	10.1	7.3	8.9	14.4	100.0

proceedings and trials, there are few trials, too, in relation to the number of cases initiated by the issuance of felony warrants. Table 2 showed that, for example, in November 1966, Recorder's Court issued 704 felony warrants, but tried only 29 cases. In Table 4, we find that in that month while 29 cases were tried, in 149 other cases defendants pleaded guilty without the formality of a trial and that 155 cases were disposed of in other ways: dismissed on motion of the prosecutor or the court, nolle prosequied or information quashed.

The inference is clear. Of all criminal cases brought to the attention of the courts—that is, where warrants are issued—only a small number come finally to trial. Totals in Table 4 show that twice as many defendants were acquitted by the court as by a jury, that twice as many were found guilty by the court as by a jury, and that four times as many defendants pleaded guilty than were actually tried.

The data in Table 4 suggests quite clearly, too, that the opportunity for influencing the outcome of a trial by pre-trial publication is somewhat restricted. Only a limited number of criminal acts result in trials and only a limited number of trials are tried before a jury. In the six-months period under study here, only 380 out of 3,051 cases were tried and of these only 129 were tried before a jury. Table 5, giving data for the calendar years of 1966 and 1967, expands somewhat on the data given in Table 4.

Tables 4 and 5 suggest that only a small number of all criminal cases originating with warrants issued by the Recorder's Court come to trial before a jury. Tables 6 and 7 suggest further that very few of the cases that come before a jury are given any newspaper publicity at all. Many stories about crimes do not include the names of suspects or defendants, as was shown in Table 3. Where suspects or defendants are named, few of the cases end in a trial before a jury.

Table 6 lists the 28 news stories appearing in the *Free Press* in November 1966, in which circumstances reported in the news story indicated that the case would fall within the jurisdiction of the Recorder's Court. Thirty-two persons were named in the 28 news stories. Of these, 26 were arraigned during the month of November. No record was found in Recorder's Court records of six persons named in the 28 stories.

Disposition of each case is summarized in Table 6. Table 7 gives a breakdown of the cases involving the 32 persons named in the 28 *Free Press* news stories. Only six of the defendants were tried before a jury. One was acquitted and five were found guilty.

If these six defendants who received newspaper publicity are

Table 4. Felony Cases Disposed of by Recorder's Court in Six Months in 1966 and 1967

	Nov.	Dec.	Jan.	Feb.	Mar.	Apr.	Total	Per cent
(1) Tried by Judge	14	26	46	47	61	57	251	8.2
Tried by Jury	15	14	9	18	41	32	129	4.2
Total Trials	29	40	55	65	102	89	380	12.4
(2) Acquitted by Judge	8	1	10	8	12	8	47	1.5
Acquitted by Jury	1	3	0	1	12	10	27	.9
Total Acquittals	9	4	10	9	24	18	74	2.4
(3) Found Guilty by Judge	7	25	36	39	49	49	205	6.7
Found Guilty by Jury	14	11	9	17	29	22	102	3.3
Total Found Guilty	21	36	45	56	78	71	307	10.0
(4) Totals (2) and (3)	29	40	55	65	102	89	380	12.4
(5) Pleaded Guilty	149	205	242	233	480	382	1,691	55.4
(6) Otherwise Disposed of*	155	179	111	218	206	111	980	32.1
Totals (Lines 4, 5, 6)	333	424	408	516	788	582	3,051	100.0

*Dismissed on motion of prosecutor; dismissed by court; nolle prosequi; information quashed.
Source: Recorder's Court Clerk, Statistics compiled for Annual reports.

Table 5. Felony cases Disposed of by Recorder's Court in Calendar Years 1966 and 1967

	1966	1967
(1) Tried by Judge	376	542
Tried by Jury	196	306
Total Trials	572	848
(2) Acquitted by Judge	60	103
Acquitted by Jury	41	34
Total Acquitals	101	187
(3) Found Guilty by Judge	316	439
Found Guilty by Jury	155	222
Total Found Guilty	471	661
(4) Totals (2) and (3)	572	848
(5) Pleaded Guilty	2,722	4,745
(6) Otherwise Disposed of*	1,816	3,547
Totals (Lines 4, 5, 6)	5,110	9,140

*Dismissed on motion of prosecutor; dismissed by court; nolle prosequi; information quashed.
Source: Recorder's Court Clerk Statistics compiled for Annual reports.

compared with the number of persons arraigned in a month, or the number tried by a jury, the amount of newspaper publicity given defendants tried by a jury seems small indeed.

Lest these data mislead, the sketchy nature of the data should be emphasized. Tables 6 and 7 represent only cases reported in the *Free Press* during a single month. The 26 persons named in the news stories were all arraigned in November, but their cases were not finally disposed of, as Table 6 shows, until far into 1967 and in several cases, 1968. These 26 defendants may have received additional publicity in stories published after the month of November, of course. However, the data in Table 3 indicates that stories originating after arraignment represent roughly one-third of all news stories of crimes and criminal trials.

Not only is the number of news stories about crimes or criminal trials fairly small, but the data presented in Tables 8 and 9 suggest that crime is not a very important part of the news budget. As Table 8 shows, the *Free Press* in the six-month period under study averaged considerably less than one crime story a day on the front page. More than one a day, but less than two, appeared on page 3A of the *Free Press*, the newspaper's second "front page." Two-thirds of all the stories about crime or criminal trials appeared on either page 2, a jump page (not a very good display page) or farther back in the paper. More than one-half of the news stories about crimes or criminal trials published during this period, as Table 9 shows, were carried under a 1-column head. A little more than one-third appeared

Table 6. Disposition of Cases in Which Suspects or Defendants Were Named in Stories Appearing in the Detroit *Free Press*, from 1 November through 30 November 1966

Date of News Story	Charge	Defendant	Disposition	Date of Disposition	Tried by	
					Judge	Jury
1 November 2	Bribery and conspiracy	Peter Vitale Anthony Kimball Charles Smith	No record[1]			
2 November 3	Assault	Mrs. Judith Peoples John Allen	Pleaded guilty	1-18-68	X	
3 November 7	Murder	Garrett Parker	Found guilty	10- 5-67		X
4 November 8	Murder	Chester S. Hall	Acquitted	4- 1-68		X
5 ”	Carrying concealed weapon	Mary S. Alli	Pleaded guilty	5-22-67		
6 ”	Murder	Garrett Parker	See above			
7 ”	Murder	William Rakestraw	Pleaded guilty	7-21-67		
8 November 9	Murder	William Rakestraw	See above			
9 November 11	Embezzlement	Charles Oakman	Dismissed on motion of prosecutor	2-15-67		
10 ”	Conspiracy to defraud	Arthur Smith Albert Ridley Thomas Harris	Dismissed on motion of prosecutor	4- 5-68		
11 November 13	Murder	Michael M. Robinson	Found guilty	12-11-67		X

Table 6 (cont'd)

	Date of News Story	Charge	Defendant	Disposition	Date	Tried by Court	Jury
12	November 13	Felonious assault	George Miller	Dismissed	1- 8-67		
			Ronald Kozanski	Dismissed	1- 8-67		
			Floyd Roach	Pleaded guilty	9- 8-67		
13	"	Carrying deadly weapon	James L. Syze	Pleaded guilty	4-28-67		
14	November 14	Murder	Michael Robinson	See above			
15	"	Murder	Charles Russell	No record[1]			
16	"	Operating blind pig	James Price	No record[1]			
17	November 15	Attempted assault	Willie Burney	Pleaded guilty	2- 7-68	X	
18	"	Felonious assault		Continued			
19	November 17	Bribery of police officer	Charles Sherman	Pleaded guilty	4- 5-68		
20	"	Attempted larceny	Robert Taylor	Motion to quash granted	2-21-67		
21	November 18	Uttering and publishing	Richard Permian	No record[1] dismissed[2]			
22	"	Murder	Mrs. Judith Peoples John Allen	See above			
23	November 21	Assault to commit murder	Joseph Kondator	Found guilty	9-22-67		X
			Juan Campion	Found guilty	9-22-67		X
			Jose Salas	Dismissed	n.d.		
			Charles Korody	Pending			
			Camilo Lopez	Found guilty	9-22-67		X

Table 6 (cont'd)

Date of News Story	Charge	Defendant	Disposition	Date	Tried by Judge	Jury
24 November 23	Assault	Wayne Walker Mike Lucci	Complaints dropped[2] No record[1]			
25 November 26	Murder	Chester Hall	See above			
26 November 28	Assault	Wayne Walker Mike Lucci	See above			
27 November 29	Assault	Wayne Walker Mike Lucci	See above			
28 "	Murder	Willie J. Harper	Pleaded guilty	8-23-67	X	

[1]Warrant issued before October 27 and not shown on File Progress Sheet examined.
[2]According to Detroit *Free Press*.
Source: File Progress Sheet compiled by Recorder's Court Clerk covering warrants issued from October 27, 1966, through December 4, 1966.
Files of Detroit *Free Press* on microfilm (held by Michigan State Library, Lansing).

under headlines ranging from two to four columns. Only 10 per cent of all stories carried headlines larger than five columns.

This study has been a limited one: one city, one newspaper, one court. The newspaper certainly isn't typical, for the *Free Press* is one of a small handful of daily newspapers with a circulation of more than 500,000. The data are suggestive, however, for the *Free Press* quite obviously does not print a great deal of news about crimes

Table 7. Disposition of Cases/Suspects Identified in *Free Press* News Stories in November, 1966, and Traceable in Court Records[1]

(1) News stories naming suspects		58
(2) Number of persons in Recorder's Court jurisdiction		32
Arraigned	26	
No record	6	
total	32	
(3) Arraigned		26
Pleaded guilty	9	
Tried	6	
Otherwise disposed of	10	
Pending	1	
total	26	
(4) Of those tried		6
Tried by judge	0	
Tried by jury	6	
Convicted by judge	0	
Convicted by jury	5	
Acquitted by judge	0	
Acquitted by jury	1	
total	6	

[1]This table summarizes data given in Table 6.
Source: Daily Record Sheet, Recorder's Court, November 1966.

Table 8. Position of News Stories in the Detroit *Free Press*, November 1, 1966–April 30, 1967

	Page 1	Page 3a	Other Inside	Total
November 1966	17	40	109	166
December 1966	12	32	115	159
January 1967	22	44	92	158
February 1967	17	30	73	120
March 1967	23	57	132	212
April 1967	22	46	105	173
Total	113	249	626	988
Percent	12.8	25.2	63.4	100.0

and criminal trials in relation to the total number of cases handled by the Detroit Recorder's Court. The data for November, 1966 suggests strongly that few cases going before a jury get any publicity at all.

Obviously, not all newspapers are alike. Further studies along the lines suggested are in order in other cities and of other newspapers. More typical newspapers might be examined, the 10,000 circulation daily, for example. Certainly some few cases in which there is extensive newspaper coverage ought to be studied in some depth. Case 23, in Table 6, is an example. This case, not a major one in terms of national interest, did get considerable coverage, and in this was not typical of most cases in Recorder's Court.

Some few criminal cases do get extensive coverage, not only locally, but nationally. Four cases outside of Michigan included in this study are probably representative. These were the Shepard retrial, the two murder trials of Dr. Carl Coppolino, the murder trial of Richard Speck, and the James Hoffa jury tampering trial. These cases inflated the figures in this study, but certainly news stories in the Detroit *Free Press* are not likely to have much effect on juries in New Jersey, Florida, Tennessee, and Illinois.

Table 9. Headline Size

		1 - Column	2 to 4 Column	5 Column and Up	Total
November	1966	91	68	7	166
December	1966	88	49	22	159
January	1967	85	59	14	158
February	1967	70	44	6	120
March	1967	109	81	22	212
April	1967	80	67	26	173
Total		523	368	97	988
Percent		52.8	37.2	9.8	100.0

... III ...

The Press, the Jury,
and the Behavioral Sciences

WALTER WILCOX

THE writer expresses his appreciation to Professors Nathan Maccoby, Institute for Communication Research, Stanford University, and William J. McGuire, Department of Psychology, University of California, San Diego, who provided valuable bibliographical advice; Dr. Chilton R. Bush, professor emeritus of communication, Stanford University, and director and founder of ANPA's News Research Center, who provided guidance, criticism and encouragement; Professors Hans Zeisel and Harry Kalven, Jr., both of the School of Law, University of Chicago, who graciously set aside time from busy schedules to lend their considerable collective insight to a discussion of problems inherent to the study; and the American Newspaper Publishers Association Foundation, which provided that welcome combination of funds and free rein.

This appreciation is in no way diminished by the customary and essential statement that the interpretations, emphases, and conclusions are the sole responsibility of the writer.

The Problem

THERE has grown in recent years a controversy between press and bar of far-reaching significance to both of these professions and the public. For each side the controversy is shaped by public values of first importance to democratic societies: on the one hand the right of the accused to a speedy and fair trial and on the other the right of the press to report fully on all public business—and the implied right of the citizen to that information. Both were of sufficient importance to the Founding Fathers to be incorporated into the Constitution as the First and Sixth Amendments.

Spectacular events have exacerbated the controversy and brought it to general public attention. The Sheppard murder trial, the Billy Sol Estes case, the two Kennedy assassinations and a multiple murder in Chicago—all are cases in point. None has so far led to a judicial answer to the question, nor have countless conferences among press, bar and bench and resolutions and guidelines by professional groups led to workable solutions.

There are clear questions of fact, however, that all sides should agree have direct bearing on the controversy: *under what conditions is pretrial publicity actually prejudicial?* If we knew enough about communications and their effects on human behavior, might we not be in a position to specify in terms acceptable within the framework of legal and journalistic ethics and practices the nature and limits of these conditions?

Empirical evidence bearing directly on the effects of pretrial publicity upon the jury verdicts is sparse. Widespread and continuous—even agonizing—efforts by bar, bench and press to search out some sort of accomodation to this perplexing issue have had few hard facts for guidance, but rather proceed on the basis of information that is largely intuitive and speculative. The bellwether Supreme Court decisions, *Irvin* v. *Dowd*, *Rideaux* v. *Louisiana* and *Sheppard* v. *Maxwell*,[1] are based on deductive assumptions; that is, the decisions turned upon the degree of prejudice that might logically be deduced from media

---

[1] *Irvin* v. *Dowd*: 81 SCt 1639 (1961); *Rideaux* v. *Louisiana*: 83 SCt 294 (1963) 83 SCt 1417 (1963); *Sheppard* v. *Maxwell*: 86 SCt 1507 (1966).

publicity. The ultimate test—whether the publicity actually did create prejudice—was beyond the scope of the facts available to the court in each instance.

Supreme Court Justice Felix Frankfurter wrote in a 1952 dissenting opinion that:

Science with all its advances has not given us instruments for determining when the impact of such newspaper exploitation has spent itself or whether the powerful impression bound to be made by such inflaming articles as here preceded the trial can be dissipated in the mind of the average juror by the tame and often pedestrian proceedings in court.[2]

In the context of the case, in which the conviction of a child murderer was upheld, "science" denoted the social or behavioral sciences, "newspaper exploitation" denoted prejudicial pretrial jublicity and "proceedings in court" denoted the jury trial. Thus, Justice Frankfurter cast into alignment the three elements central to the question: *Does pretrial publicity indeed have a scientifically measurable effect upon jury verdicts?* Or, stated with more caution: "Do some kinds of pretrial publicity under some kinds of conditions have some kinds of influence upon some kinds of jurors with a scientifically measurable effect upon jury verdicts?"

The objective of the present review is not to provide a definitive answer to this question; no such answer exists. Rather it aspires to a three-way linkage of the segments to determine if indeed existing behavioral science theories, concepts, principles, postulates and experiments have the power to illuminate the question of fair trial *v.* free press and, if so, the extent of such power. This review assumes the reader is familiar with the fair trial/free press dialogue, with its often heated partisanship and repetition to the point where a kind of *deja vu* effect has set in. The review is objective in the sense that it purposely rules out an evaluation of subjective judgments and in the sense that it takes no position on the issue itself .

Definitions

In the interest of efficient discussion the three elements are assigned definitive descriptions as follows:

Behavioral Science. This term may be defined simply as the scien-

---

[2] *Stroble* v. *California*: 343 U.S. 181 (1952).

tific study of behavior, in this case human behavior; it was chosen over "social science" as more precise because the latter term includes disciplines as extraneous to this review as history. In the present context, the term is narrowed to embrace chiefly that sector dealing with the effects of communication upon images, perceptions, attitudes and behaviors. The attitude sector alone is one of formidable size and complexity. For example, the chapter on "The Nature of Attitudes and Attitude Change" in the forthcoming *Handbook of Social Psychology* includes approximately 850 references, most of which report experimental studies.

In order to place the behavioral sciences in juxtaposition with the other two elements (pretrial publicity and jury trial) it is necessary to relate the scientific terms to their lay equivalents. Typically, in the interest of experimental management, manipulation and control, the student of attitudes divides the phenomenon of attitude into three components. These components are not discrete in the sense that one has no effect on the other; they are interrelated and the division is an arbitrary one. Following is a translation from the scientific term to the lay term, together with its behavioral counterpart:

	Components		
Scientific Term	Cognitive	Affective	Conative
Lay Terms	Perceiving/learning/ remembering/thinking	Feeling	Seeking/ acting
Behavior	Intellectual (covert)	Emotional	Active (overt)

The fit is not precise. Knowing and feeling may be independent or may correlate highly. There may or may not be emotional reaction (feeling) to news (knowing) of a shocking murder. The acting component is not parallel to the others and figures here chiefly in the overt acts of debating and voting the jury verdict. Decision making behavior, individually or in groups, involves all three components.

The scientific terms are used in this review because they are more precise. ("Knowing," for instance, does not necessarily carry the notion of intellectual behavior.) These "constructs" are further defined in the context of the discussion.

A typical attitude experiment based on the "before-after" design is outlined here for the case of a hypothetical study of the effects of a persuasive communication on attitudes toward flouridation: 1) *Sub-*

jects, a selected and usually quite homogeneous group, often undergraduate students, are randomly assigned to "experimental" and "control" conditions. 2) *Before Test*—Attitudes toward flouridation are elicited by means of a testing instrument. 3) *Manipulation*—Experimental groups are exposed to a message or messages; for example, they might be exposed to a pro-flouridation or an anti-flouridation message by a high credibility source such as a public health official or a low credibility source such as a faith healer. Control groups are given no message or an innocuous or irrelevant message. 4) *After Test*—Experimental groups are tested for attitude change in comparison with the control group and the resulting differences are subjected to statistical inference to determine whether differences of such magnitude and variability could have been obtained by chance. Within this scheme it is possible to introduce variables of various kinds to test a whole series of hypotheses; for example, the order of presentation of the pro and con arguments, strength of argument, forewarning that an opposite argument is forthcoming, etc.[3]

Pretrial publicity: The two attitudinal components involved here are cognitive and affective. It is logical to assume that the newspaper reader is exposed to the cognitive component through the newspaper coverage of a crime and relevant detail, and it is logical to assume the affective component comes into play at the same time. But the conative component—the actual decision behavior produced by such stories—still is highly speculative. Unfortunately, these must for the present time remain assumptions, albeit powerful ones. To paraphrase Justice Frankfurter, communication research with all its advances and sophistication has not given us instruments to determine precisely the impact of a crime story upon the reader in terms of knowing and feeling, let alone acting.

No operational definition of pretrial publicity has been widely agreed upon. Until this has happened it is more appropriately cast in the form of a cluster centered upon the crime and the accused, in the manner of the schematic diagram in Figure 1.

This rather elaborate scheme is set forth to emphasize the complexity of pretrial publicity when aligned against the cognitive and affective components of attitude. The linkages indicated by the lines, some of

[3] More likely than not the scientist is interested in hypotheses such as these and not in fluoridation as such. He would be likely to use several such topics, in fact, to eliminate any effects of the unique features of one particular issue.

FIGURE 1

Communication System: Pretrial Publicity

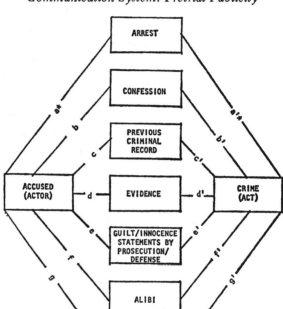

* The lines denote linkages between successive events (which frequently result in pretrial news coverage) and the accused on the one hand (*a, b*) and the crime on the other, (a′, b′). Each linkage carries the possibility of an attitudinal linkage in the minds of readers (and potential jurors).

** Elements under "other" are too numerous to list and probably can never be exhaustive. Crime news stories have included: 1) Psychological state of the accused at the time of arrest, 2) Previous deviant behavior of the accused as elicited from relatives and acquaintances, 3) Analogies with previous crimes, 4) Imagery such as "Fang Suspect," 5) Massive imbalance of accusation over alibi, 6) Emphasis on the penalty for the crime, 7) Detail of questionable relevance such as race, foreign birth, physical peculiarities, etc.

which may be clear and unequivocal (e.g., arrest) and others of which may be highly circumstantial (e.g., speculation about guilt or innocence) indicate those variables the presence and relative strength of which make up the configuration of pretrial publicity. In order to make the definition operationally complete several dimensions must be added.

In the absence of directly relevant research, these dimensions must be cast in the form of propositions:

¶ *Celebrated cases will contain more elements from the pretrial publicity configuration than routine cases, and consequently will attract greater attention.* Celebrated in this sense may be defined pragmatically by the degree of space allotted by the press, or more subjectively, according to the presence or absence of: prominence of the accused and/ or the victim, overtones of sexual conflict, horror, fascination, brutality, etc., in multiple combinations. At the other end of the continuum, the routine case is often a simple, sometimes sordid, act of violence by a comparatively unknown person. This proposition, then, merely links together the common assumptions with respect to news values: high interest/high news value/high coverage.[4]

¶ *Metropolitan newspapers employ different news value criteria than community newspapers.* Typically, the metropolitan newspaper concentrates upon the celebrated case; its scope is horizontal, seeking out the celebrated case for extensive treatment and giving only perfunctory treatment, or none at all, to the routine case. Conversely, the community newspaper covers all cases of record; its scope is vertical in that it penetrates much more deeply into the local news than does the metropolitan paper. In addition, it has fewer resources for investigative reporting and typically it cannot explore the celebrated case in as much detail as can the metropolitan newspaper. As a further complication, many readers are exposed both to the metropolitan newspaper and the community newspaper. In the celebrated case, the metropolitan newspaper will invade the community newspaper's coverage area, and thus locale of the case becomes a factor.

Cast in terms of the opportunity for reader exposure, the possibilities include at least 15 conditions, ranging from *celebrated case, community locale, reader subscribes to both newspapers,* down through a variety of combinations to *routine case, metropolitan locale, crime not reported.*

---

[4] This discussion deliberately ignores what might be called the "super celebrated case"—the assassinations of John F. Kennedy, Martin Luther King, Jr., and Robert F. Kennedy. These cases, while the focus of much attention upon the fair trial/free press issue, are highly atypical; they are, in effect, national events of which the crime is only a part.

¶ *The presence and/or strength of the linkage* (a-a^1, b-b^1, etc.) *establishes a scale of manifest guilt and this scale measures the relative presence or absence of the prejudicial dimension.* Further, the prejudicial dimension is introduced when an element is present in the pretrial story but does not emerge in the jury trial (e.g., a confession is ruled inadmissible). It should be emphasized that in this discussion actual prejudice is not assumed.

This review has chosen to ignore any distinction between anti-defendant pretrial publicity and pro-defendant pretrial publicity for two reasons. First, the behavioral science material itself makes no such distinction; it usually probes both ways. Second, that era when the press lionized the accused with sympathetic coverage has long passed.

Jury Trial

The American jury system has generated a massive body of literature centered upon legal philosophy, such as use of the layman in the administration of justice, and upon pragmatic functionalism, such as the just verdict. The definitional description here must confine itself to a specific aspect of the latter: the effect of pretrial publicity on the just verdict. Also, it is necessary to cast the jury trial structure in a form amenable to study in terms of attitude change in relation to pretrial publicity. This structure is given in diagramatic form in Figure 2.

Exposure refers to the nature and impact of pretrial publicity upon the prospective juror and covers the period from the first news reports to selection of the jury panel. The exposure stimulus ranges from a large number of stories in a celebrated case to one simple crime and arrest story in a routine case.

Jury Selection: Venire, the process of empanelling a jury, is allotted a separate segment (as opposed to *voir dire,* or questioning of the jury panel members) because it is quite possible that a person chosen from among his fellows to perform a solemn task of citizenship may well change in some manner as a consequence. For instance, he might, consciously or otherwise, reevaluate the information (Exposure) about the crime and the accused.

Jury Selection: Voir Dire, while a part of the jury selection process, is allotted a separate segment because it is here that exposure to pretrial publicity first confronts the formal jury process. "Have you read about this case in the newspapers? Discussed it with anyone? Do you

FIGURE 2

Schematic Structure: Exposure and Jury Trial

Exposure*	Jury Selection: Venire	Jury Selection: Voir Dire	Trial Arguments	Admonition	Deliberation	Verdict
†A ⟶	⟶	⟶	⟶	⟶	⟶	⟶
B ⟶	⟶	⟶	⟶	⟶	⟶	
C ⟶	⟶	⟶	⟶	⟶		
D ⟶	⟶	⟶	⟶			
E ⟶	⟶	⟶				
F ⟶	⟶					
G ⟶						

* Headings represent the sequence of events in the exposure-trial process.

† Letters represent messages: arrest, confession, etc., as in Figure 1.

honestly think you can strike this from your mind?" Etc. It is reasonable to assume that *voir dire* may have two effects: 1) the direct effect of eliminating a juror who in the view of the prosecution or defense is prejudiced by pretrial publicity, or 2) the indirect effect of reenforcing his resolution to reevaluate the exposure or put it out of mind.

Trial Arguments embrace the following as set forth by Bush:[5]

Opening statement of the prosecution.

Presentation of the prosecution's evidence by direct, cross-, and redirect examination.

Opening statement of the defense; this statement is sometimes made after the prosecution's opening statement.

Presentation of defendant's evidence.

Presentation of rebuttal evidence, if any, by both parties.

Summation by both parties.

Judge's instructions to the jury.

This stage of the trial finds its counterpart in the pretrial publicity model chiefly under evidence (Fig. 1). Certainly, evidence in a trial is

[5] Chilton R. Bush, *Newswriting and Reporting Public Affairs* (Philadelphia: Chilton Books, 1965), p. 353.

not isolated in pristine objectivity; rather it is heavily embedded in a persuasive context. In essence, it is covered by both the cognitive and affective components of attitude, with each side striving to maximize or minimize the strength of these variables. This segment spans that portion of the trial procedure in which arguments are developed; it is the main event of the trial.

Three conditions are relevant to the evidence as related to pretrial publicity: 1) evidence described in pretrial publicity that does not emerge in court (for example, a confession ruled inadmissible); 2) evidence described in pretrial publicity and also introduced at the trial, which may be altered or refuted or sustained in the context of the trial arguments, and 3) evidence introduced in court but not mentioned in pretrial publicity. The last is of limited relevance to the present review; it would be of concern only if it changes the direction of the trial to the point where the first two conditions become irrelevant.

Admonition in the context used here denotes the admonition by the judge to the jury in the *preventive cautionary instructions* (a legal term): "You are not to consider any matters other than evidence presented at the trial." Again, such admonition may hypothetically be presumed to have an effect under two conditions: 1) manifest suppression of pretrial publicity as when one juror has read about a confession and the other 11 members have not, presuming the one juror responds properly to the admonition and 2) latent suppression, as in the situations hypothesized under jury selection; that is, the juror makes an effort, conscious or otherwise, to strike the extraneous matter from his mind.

Deliberation in the context of this review impinges upon another specific subdivision of the behavioral sciences: small group communication and interaction. Legally, the deliberation stage of a trial denotes the consensus-reaching procedure. But in the scientific context, it involves an added dimension. In the simple sense of cognitive/affective/conative behavior the individual is considered in isolation; that is, in many experiments of the before/after format, the subjects have no lateral communication among themselves, although this variable has been introduced in a number of experiments. The trial jury deliberation is a classic example of the artificially-created (as opposed to voluntary) small group in a problem solving setting wherein persuasive influence may be exerted. Both its number and composition are frozen, its task is clearly defined and its communication intake is, ideally, controlled. But in the legal tradition the jury room is an inviolate sanctuary. Only through inference can the interaction of attitude, persuasion and personality be studied.

Verdict is the single clear and unequivocal segment in the trial process that can be aligned against its behavioral science counterpart—decision making behavior. Whereas in the other sectors of the trial process cognitive and affective components are mixed, in the verdict the overt act—guilty/not guilty/hung jury—is manifest, establishing a one-for-one relationship. It is what behavioral scientists call the dependent variable—the ultimate test of the effect of prejudicial pretrial publicity.

The letters in the pretrial publicity diagram (Fig. 2) represent messages and the arrows the hypothetical progress of the message through the sequence. *A*, for instance, may be the report of a previous criminal record that, unimpeded, continues through the verdict segment. *G*, on the other hand, hypothetically may be the report of a confession that is resolutely set aside by the venireman at the first barrier. *E* may be cut off at the evidence stage by adverse testimony, *D* by the judge's admonition, etc.

The neatness of the model is of course illusory; it merely provides a simple framework for discussion and points of reference for application of the relevant behavioral science experiments.

Problems of Alignment

Hypothetically, pretrial publicity has or does not have an effect upon the jury trial and behavioral science does or does not illuminate the processes involved.

It might be argued that both the jury trial and behavioral science have their "proof systems" in common, that both employ evidence as the basis for making an inference. But in some ways the differences are more striking than the similarities. Behavioral scientists erect theories, usually on the basis of a previous cumulation of evidence, generate hypotheses from the theory by the use of deductive logic and then test these hypotheses by designing experiments which are capable of giving them a clear answer to the question whether the data in this case lend support to the hypothesis. The data either support or disconfirm the hypothesis. By means of statistical tests based on probability theory it is possible to determine what likelihood there is that such a result could have been obtained by chance. But even when the results are clearly significant by such test, the experimenter is cautious in his interpretation and typically chary of generalizing beyond the results obtained.

Conversely, the proof system for the trial jury is highly subjective. The "beyond a reasonable doubt" test is the product of many variables, none of which may be measured with precision. How, then, can the two proof systems be meaningfully aligned? Is it tenable to assume that the ".05 level of confidence" test for the experimenter equivalent to the "beyond a reasonable doubt" test for the trial jury? The answer must be equivocal: with warning flags flying and the avenues of retreat wide open, it may be assumed that the proofs are roughly equivalent under the very different rules of evidence each one plays,[6] all other factors being under control. For example, if an experimenter demonstrates that a confession remains measurably more potent in the minds of his subjects than a subsequent repudiation of that confession, it is reasonable to assume the same is generally true of jurors, *subject to other variables*. In short, while the two proof systems differ in detail, they answer to an equivalent sort of pragmatic logic. This does not mean that a one-for-one relationship exists between the experiment and real life.

In pretrial publicity, the proof system is one of factual empiricism; hence it is necessary to cast the proof system in terms of propositions. Pretrial publicity may conveniently be divided into two forms. In the first, the press itself functions as the proof object. "The wife of an electrical contractor and her male companion were shot and killed in a Northside tavern early today, police reported." In this form, the attribution is a stylistic or legalistic device; the proof object remains the newspaper, as if "the paper said . . ." is part of each statement. At the other end of the continuum the source functions as the proof object. When a defense attorney says, "My client remembers nothing; his mind is a complete blank," the press is in effect a common carrier. Hence, the proof system is variable, ranging from high credibility when the material is factual and the press is the proof object, to relatively low credibility when the material is speculative and the source is the proof object. Cast into a schematic diagram the proof system emerges as a four-cell contingency table:

Proof Object	Factual	Speculative
Press	High Credibility	Variable Credibility
Source	Variable Credibility	Low Credibility

[6] For a discussion of this point, consult Daniel Lerner, ed., *Evidence and Inference* (Glencoe, Illinois: The Free Press, 1958).

This framework, although based upon an untested assumption, provides a guide to pretrial publicity in its various forms as may affect the belief systems of prospective jurors.

Notes on Method

The research technique used in this review was uncomplicated. It consisted in: 1) analysis of four studies bearing directly upon the problem, 2) a survey of previous studies relating the behavioral sciences to the jury trial and 3) a survey of relevant behavioral science literature. This involved identification of pertinent study clusters (e.g., open/closed mind, selective exposure, cognitive dissonance, credibility, inoculation, etc.) and review and evaluation of relevant experiments and conceptual reviews. This step was both time consuming and inefficient. Normally, such a review would concentrate upon anthologies, textbooks and academic journal summaries on the assumption that the significant studies would survive and minor or peripheral studies would fall by the way. However, in this case the object of the search may well have been hidden as a by-product of the experiment; secondary sources or summaries may have omitted a portion of the experiment relevant to the search. Further, it was often impossible to determine the relevance of a study from the title, or from a synopsis in a journal of abstracts or from the context of a citation. Hence, it was necessary to seek out some 300 individual reports, the great majority of which were of little or no value. The search was considered complete when, having come full circle, the footnotes cited material previously reviewed. In the end it was found that most of the relevant material is contained in four volumes, Jones and Gerard, Insko, Berelson and Steiner and Kalven and Zeisel.[7] In addition, the manuscript for the chapter on "The Nature of Attitudes and Attitude Change" in the forthcoming revised *Handbook of Social Psychology* was made available by William J. McGuire and provided a valuable source from which to seek out others. How exhaustive the search actually was cannot be answered here except as may be inferred from the above. Undoubtedly, some thesis on a library shelf, some report in the academic journal of a related discipline, some on-going

[7] Bernard Berelson and Gary A. Steiner, *Human Behavior* (New York: Harcourt Brace and World, 1964); Chester A. Insko, *Theories of Attitude Change* (New York: Appleton-Century-Crofts, 1967); Edward E. Jones and Harold B. Gerard, *Foundations of Social Psychology* (New York: John Wiley, 1967); Harry Kalven, Jr., and Hans Zeisel, *The American Jury* (Boston: Little, Brown, 1966).

study, failed to turn up. But the law of diminishing returns intruded all too early as it was.

The resulting data defy elegant quantitative analysis or even a systematic qualitative one. Each behavioral science concept was examined for relevance and tested against common sense; then an attempt was made to give it perspective in the cause-and-effect linkage that is the framework for this report.

Four Experiments on Point

THE LEGAL BASTION erected by the courts against direct research into the effects of pretrial publicity upon the jury is apparently impervious. In 1954, researchers working on the University of Chicago Jury Project, a massive study sponsored by the Ford Foundation, recorded a jury deliberation in a civil case with the permission of the judge and the litigants. The recorded transcript, designed as an instrument to gain insights into patterns of the deliberation, was played to some 200 trial judges attending a conference. For a time nothing happened, but some three months later, a story in the Los Angeles *Times* triggered a national furor. The sanctity of the jury room had been compromised. The incident culminated in an investigation by the Senate Subcommittee on Internal Security.[1]

While the sanctions against research into an on-going trial appear to be impregnable, post-trial interviews of jurors have been conducted from time to time. But the attitude of the judiciary, while not necessarily unanimous, is succinctly expressed in a 1948 court decision: "He who makes studied inquiries of jurors as to what occurred there acts at his peril, lest he be held as acting in obstruction of the administration of justice."[2]

Faced with this formidable barrier to direct access, the researcher must rely upon the simulated situation. Four such studies have been reported. Two traced the process from exposure through verdict, and the other two dealt only with the exposure of prospective jurors. These four studies are outlined below.

[1] Donald M. Gillmor, "Free Press and Fair Trial: A Continuing Dialogue. Trial by Newspaper and the Social Sciences," *North Dakota Law Review*, 38: 672–88 (1965).

[2] *Ibid.*

63

Simon

Rita Simon, associate professor of sociology at the University of Illinois, and her colleagues conducted a "pilot study" with adult mock jurors.[3]

Question: Are juries really prejudiced by pretrial news reports?

Subjects: 97 persons from the list of registered voters in Champaign and Urbana, Illinois, representing those who volunteered from 825 registered voters approached. The demographic profile was biased in the direction of upper middle class.

Variables: 1) A "sensational" version of a pretrial publicity sequence of three stories (woman killed, two arrested, murder weapon found); this version was described in the study "as the sensational tabloids would handle it," with gory details, blatant headlines, etc.; 2) a "conservative" story series, described "as it would be played by a conservative paper like the New York *Times*." The sensational version emphasized the previous criminal record, whereas—although not stated explicitly—it is assumed the conservative version did not. At a meeting, 51 mock jurors were exposed to the sensational version and 56 to the conservative version. (The discrepancy between 97 and 107 subjects is not explained.)

Procedure: 1) Subjects were asked to read the stories and then to ballot on guilt or innocence, 2) subjects were then exposed to a recording of an abbreviated trial consisting of an admonition from the judge, open statements, testimony from witnesses, closing statements and instructions from the judge; 3) jurors were once more asked to vote on the guilt or innocence of the accused men.

Results: The figures for the principal defendant (previous criminal record) and for the co-defendant (presumably no criminal record) are given in Table 1.

The results indicate quite dramatically the power of the jury trial to overcome the effects of sensationalism and of the report of a previous criminal record.

Critique: The study has the limitations common to such research, especially the artificial setting and an atypical (self-selective) sample. The nature and potency of the within-trial communications (testimony, instructions, etc.) are not stipulated, nor do we know that they were

[3] Rita James Simon, "Murder, Juries and the Press," *Trans-Action*, May–June, 1966.

TABLE 1

Result of Balloting on Guilt, Before and After Trial
by Two Conditions of Pre-Trial Publicity
(Data from Simon)

| | | % Guilty | | % Not Guilty | | % No Opinion | |
		Before Trial	After Trial	Before Trial	After Trial	Before Trial	After Trial
Sensational	Criminal Record	67	25	21	73	12	2
	No Criminal Record	53	25	33	73	14	2
Conservative	Criminal Record	37	22	39	78	24	..
	No Criminal Record	37	22	39	78	24	..

controlled. There was no control (unexposed) group against which to measure effects.

Significance: The study shows that sensational press treatment can enhance jurors' readiness to believe the defendant guilty before trial, and the more so the more the publicity pointed to a criminal record. *But it also shows that experience of the trial itself can reduce such effects to the vanishing point.* It also is noteworthy that those who saw a conservative press treatment were less willing than those who saw a sensational press treatment to make a judgment before trial; these differences, too, disappeared after trial.

Kline and Jess

F. Gerald Kline, fellow in the Research Division of the School of Journalism at the University of Minnesota, and Paul H. Jess, assistant professor of journalism at South Dakota State University, conducted a mock jury study.[4]

Hypothesis: Prejudicial news stories carried by both printed and electronic media affect the jury in a simple civil case.

[4] F. Gerald Kline and Paul H. Jess, "Prejudicial Publicity: Its Effects on Law School Mock Juries," *Journalism Quarterly*, 43:113–16 (1966).

Subjects: 48 male sophomores divided into two groups and equated for college entrance scores and age.

Variables: "Prejudicial" and "non-prejudicial" versions of a traffic injury represented as a story run in the university daily newspaper and inserted in a simulated newscast. The prejudicial element involved a deplorable driving record, including arrests for drunken driving, reckless driving and leaving the scene of an accident.

Procedure: 1) Subjects were exposed to the stories and to the newscasts under camouflage conditions, 2) subjects were divided into eight 6-man juries, 3) one control (non-prejudicial exposure) and one experimental (prejudicial exposure) were assigned to each of four law school mock jury trials presided over by actual judges, 4) after the trial presentation and the judge's instruction, the juries were divided according to exposure and assigned to jury rooms that were linked by hidden microphones to a tape recorder, 5) the subjects were given tests for authoritarianism (California F-Scale)[5] and for open/closed mindedness, using a shortened form of the Rokeach Dogmatism Scale.[6]

Results: 1) At least one member of each of the "prejudiced" juries made reference to the defendant's driving record, but 2) in three of the four juries, subjects decided not to make use of the prejudicial material; analysis of the transcript revealed that this decision was based to a great extent on the judge's instructions, which were described as standardized, 3) in these three cases, the juries found for the defendant; the experimenters concluded that other factors not under control (e.g., power of argument, affinity of a student jury for a student defendant) operated to explain the decision, 4) in the fourth case, the experimental jury found for the plaintiff, basing part of its rationale on the prejudicial material.[7] In sum, the experimenters found some evidence that pretrial publicity retained a measure of potency through the trial procedure to the deliberation; in three of four cases it was cut off before the verdict stage, due largely to the judge's instructions; only in the fourth case did

---

[5] T. W. Adorno, *et al., The Authoritarian Personality* (New York: Harper & Bros., 1950).

[6] Milton Rokeach, *The Open and Closed Mind* (New York: Basic Books, 1960).

[7] The findings on the effects of authoritarianism and dogmatism are not summarized here because they are inconclusive and the discussion was highly speculative.

it figure in the verdict itself. The design of the study did not permit the usual tests of signifiance, however.

Critique: Ideally, the ultimate test within this model would be a simple measure of guilt or innocence in relation to prejudicial or non-prejudicial news story stimuli. Unfortunately, the potency and nature of the trial arguments were beyond the control of the experimenters, as the procedure was designed to double as an exercise for law students. As in the Simon study, the relative potency of the trial arguments was not accounted for. The generality of the results is further limited by two other factors. The simulated situation, especially the choice of college sophomores as subjects, strains the tenuous linkage between experiment and reality. To this strain must be added the difference between a simple civil case and a serious criminal case. On balance, the strain is too great. Finally, the results are highly tenuous because they must be based on the significance of "three cases out of four," etc.

Significance: There is some evidence that pretrial publicity can survive the procedure of a simulated jury trial if not subjected to attack. To this might be added the proposition that the potency is diminished at the end of the journey, as indicated by the ability of most jurors to set it aside. However, the latter proposition is weakened by the nature of the subjects and the setting; students may well be more responsive to cautionary instructions than others and in this case may have reverted to the role of student in responding to the judge.

Tans and Chaffee

Mary Dee Tans, then a senior at the University of Wisconsin, and Steven H. Chaffee, then assistant professor and Mrs. Tans' adviser, presented data on an experiment conducted by Mrs. Tans as her undergraduate honors thesis.[8]

Hypothesis: Pre-judgment of guilt is affected by the amount and kind of information given the prospective juror.

Subjects: 150 members of various social and work groups, including PTA, League of Women Voters, steelworkers' wives, a university extension class and other meeting groups. The total sample differed from jurors mainly in being more highly educated and composed of more females.

[8] Mary Dee Tans and Steven H. Chaffee, "Pretrial Publicity and Juror Prejudice," *Journalism Quarterly*, 43:647–54 (1966).

Variables: Three brief, fictitious newspaper stories about crimes (burglary, assault-robbery, kidnap-murder), mentioning the name of a suspect. The bodies of the stories were neutrally written and paragraphs were added to the basic story in various combinations, containing statements that would be favorable or damaging to the suspect, concerning whether 1) he had confessed or denied the charges, 2) was considered guilty or not by the district attorney and 3) had been arrested. The versions were systematically varied so that readers got different versions. There were 15 versions of each story, some containing as many as three added elements of "negative" or "positive" information.

Procedure: Each subject read three different stories, representing three of the fifteen combinations. Subjects were then asked to evaluate the suspect on a 7-point guilt-innocence scale with an option for no opinion. The scale was imbedded in a series of other scales in order to avoid singling it out for special attention.

Results: The average guilt rating on the 7-point scale for all unfavorable versions was 5.7 (7.0 being guilty) and for all favorable versions 2.9, a quite dramatic difference. The unfavorable version scores did not differ appreciably from the score for the control version (5.5) in which the suspect was "detained" or "questioned." The most damaging statement was the confession, the most benign the fact that the suspect had not been arrested, when combined with a statement by the district attorney doubtful of the suspect's guilt. In sum, the data confirmed the hypothesis.

The study explored other facets: 1) belief in guilt (and hence the unfavorable stimuli) correlated with the negative evaluations of "bad," "dumb" and "dishonest"; in short, the affective component of the attitudinal mix was apparently operative; 2) the more information available, the more the subjects were willing to judge, and 3) judgment was not materially affected by demographic variables (court experience, education, age, sex, occupation).

Chaffee, in commenting upon the study, pointed out to the author that the willingness to prejudge should become an increasingly crucial variable the closer the situation comes to real jury duty. "My hypothesis is . . . the more the person knows about the case as a juror, the more likely he is to suspend judgment until he's heard all the facts; I'd expect the reverse pattern for non-jurors."[9]

[9] In a letter to the writer dated June 28, 1968.

Critique: The limitations are best described by the authors. The subjects were not members of an actual jury and hence the results must be considered in the simulated context, particularly the fact that no appreciable time elapsed between exposure and judgment. Nevertheless, the methodology is straightforward, the variables under control and the interpretation realistic.

Significance: The study provides strong evidence that potential jurors may be influenced by the kinds of facts that are frequently found in pretrial publicity (the fact of arrest, previous convictions, authoritative assertions as to guilt, etc.) and that the more such information is given the more likely it will lead to belief in guilt. But it did not, as did the two studies previously reported here, determine the fate of such belief in the face of trial proceedings, e.g. the effects of hearing evidence and the judge's admonition to disregard information not admissible as evidence.

Wilcox and McCombs

Walter Wilcox, professor of journalism at the University of California at Los Angeles, and Maxwell McCombs, assistant professor of journalism at the University of North Carolina, probed the way prospective jurors absorb three kinds of pretrial news-story elements and how they organized them in terms of belief in innocence or guilt.[10]

Question: How do prospective jurors organize crime story elements in terms of belief in guilt or innocence?

Subjects: 120 persons drawn randomly from the list of registered voters in the 26th Congressional District of California (Los Angeles) were divided into eight matched groups of 15 subjects each.

Variables: A news story describing the arrest of a murder suspect and a brief recapitulation of the crime was manipulated by adding various combinations of three elements: confession, evidence and previous criminal record, resulting in eight versions, including control, as shown under results below.

Procedure: 1) Subjects were exposed to the front page of a laboratory newspaper containing the experimental story and other items; 2) they were then given a five-item questionnaire that included a 0–100 point scale on the guilt/innocence of the suspect; 3) next, they were interviewed with questions designed to explore the way in which they organized the material in arriving at the guilt/innocence decision.

[10] Walter Wilcox and Maxwell McCombs, "Crime Story Elements and Fair Trial/Free Press," unpublished report, University of California at Los Angeles, 1967.

TABLE 2

Average Guilt Ratings by Story Versions

Version	Score (0–100)*
Confession/criminal record	76‡
Confession/criminal record/evidence	68†
Confession	66†
Evidence	57
Control	56
Confession/evidence	56
Criminal record	50
Criminal record/evidence	39

* Numerals are the average guilt rating on a 100-point scale; the higher the score, the greater the subject's belief in the guilt of the suspect.

† By statistical tests, these scores are higher than the scores below beyond pure chance (greater than .05 level of confidence).

‡ This score was higher, statistically, than all other scores.

Results: The results are given in Table 2.

As in the Tans-Chaffee study, the confession loomed as the most potent prejudicial element, particularly in combination with criminal record.

Results for the other elements are somewhat baffling. The evidence and criminal record elements, by themselves or in combination, had no effect as a predictor of belief in guilt. The researchers speculated that the confession might be perceived as a message from the suspect himself, rather than from police authorities, hence its potency. In a test for intensity of readership of the story, the subjects spontaneously recalled confession, evidence and criminal record about equally, and the experimenters concluded intensity was not a factor. In a test for the subjects' ability to discriminate between accusation and guilt, the data were analyzed for recall of attribution (police said, charged with, etc.), with the result shown in Table 3.

As the table shows, many subjects were unable to make the distinction between accusation and guilt, as inferred from recall of attribution. Further, those unable to make the distinction are prone to a snap decision toward guilt. This suggests that it may be profitable to study the influence of individual differences among jurors in the ways they respond to pretrial publicity.

In a third test the discrimination variable was related to exposure to the confession. No measurable relationship emerged, leading the experi-

TABLE 3

*Belief in Guilt, by Individual Ability to Discriminate
Between Accusation and Guilt*

Subject Types	High Belief in Guilt	No Opinion	Low Belief in Guilt
Discriminators	16	15	21
Noncommittals	19	12	7
Non-Discriminators	17	10	1

menters to conclude that the confession is a sufficiently powerful element to cut through the factors that make for discrimination.

Critique: The limitations of the study, as expressed by the experimenters themselves, center upon the weaknesses inherent in a simulated situation (the setting was the home rather than the jury room, etc.) and the penurious structure of the experiment (only one news story topic, and this concerned with a routine rather than a celebrated case, etc.)

Significance: This study lends support to the Tans-Chaffee finding with respect to the potency of the confession. Further, it demonstrates the variability of a difference of potential importance—how prospective jurors organize pretrial publicity. The findings based on the recall data indicate that the feeling (affective) element in the attitudinal mix looms large for a substantial number of prospective jurors, and that for these jurors attributions such as "police said" are ineffective.

* * *

The four studies must be considered as the first groping efforts to unravel the effects of pretrial publicity. As direct answers to the question, "Does pretrial publicity affect jury verdicts?" they fall short of the mark. Neither do the four add up to a whole greater than the sum of the parts; the dimensions measured are too diffuse, the experimental instruments too diverse. But the parts themselves may be salvaged. Cast as propositions, these parts are: 1) sensationalism in pretrial publicity has immediate effects, but they seem to be dissipated in the trial procedure, 2) the report of a confession looms as the single most potent pretrial publicity news element and 3) the cognitive component of pretrial publicity has a certain survival capacity in the trial process.

Three Early Studies

Two studies—both content analyses—are mentioned here only in brief and for the record because: 1) they concern one case each only and are of limited generality, 2) they are relatively inconclusive, 3) they are somewhat dated and 4) they are not strictly on point. A third study—a public opinion survey—is discussed in some detail because it illustrates the complexity that is to be expected in applying one of the basic tools of public opinion research to the question of pretrial publicity.

¶ Martin Millspaugh[11] analyzed four Baltimore newspapers for biased coverage in the case of a Negro accused of the murder of a white girl. He concluded that the three white-oriented papers loaded the content against the accused and that the Negro newspaper was sympathetic.

¶ Joseph T. Klapper and Charles Y. Glock[12] analyzed the coverage by the New York City press of the loyalty investigation of Dr. Edward U. Condon, then director of the National Bureau of Standards. The results showed a preponderance of statements in favor of Condon, with four newspapers apparently favorable and five unfavorable. The authors were concerned because the unfavorable newspapers kept repeating the

TABLE 4

Views of the Guilt of Alger Hiss, New York and Rutland, Vermont

	New York (N=206)	Rutland (N=186)
Has opinion: "Guilty"	22%	23%
Has opinion: "Innocent"	12	6
Has opinion: "Won't Say"	11	5
Total with opinion	45%	34%
No opinion: undecided	28%	22%
No opinion: no knowledge	27	44
Total with no opinion	55%	66%

[11] Martin Millspaugh, "Trial by Mass Media?" *Public Opinion Quarterly*, 13: 328–9 (1949).

[12] Joseph T. Klapper and Charles Y. Glock, "Trial by Newspaper," *Scientific American*, 180:1621 (1949).

original charges of disloyalty. This, of course, did not involve a jury trial but rather a government loyalty hearing. (Condon was cleared.)

¶ A public opinion survey was taken in the course of the Alger Hiss case in support of a motion for a change of venue from New York to Rutland, Vermont, after the first trial resulted in a hung jury.[13] The defense sought to introduce the results shown in Table 4.

The prosecution attacked the survey, apparently with success, on the grounds the sample was inadequate, especially when divided into the smaller cells. However, even assuming the sample is adequate, the data are not sufficient for conclusions. First, they do not withstand statistical tests except for that proportion of respondents who had not heard about the case or paid no attention. Second, they can be interpreted in two ways: those exposed to *more* publicity are inclined to yield the benefit of the doubt because they know more about the case; conversely, those who are exposed to *less* publicity are, similarly, inclined to yield the benefit of the doubt because they know less about the case. Third, the amount and nature of the publicity was not stipulated, i.e., quantity does not equate potency and, in fact, the heavy coverage in New York City could well have been less prejudiced than the condensed coverage reaching Rutland. Fourth, some Rutland residents read New York newspapers but the sample was too small to justify reporting results for them separately. As a measure of pretrial publicity it misses the mark, involving as it does, pretrial, trial and post-trial publicity.

[13] *U.S.* v. *Hiss.* (See references.)

Two Pioneering Reviews

W HEN MR. JUSTICE FRANKFURTER complained that science has not provided the instruments with which to determine the impact of pretrial publicity, he was not precisely on target. Perhaps he should have said science has not demonstrated the application of those instruments that are available. Certainly, they have never been adequately tested.

Two 1965 reviews pertinent to the problem are summarized below. No attempt is made here to give complete detail, as the relevant studies cited are also examined in this review; nor is a critical evaluation essayed, as the reviews were designed to be provocative and exploratory rather than as definitive.

Gillmor

Donald M. Gillmor poses the question: "What *is* the effect of trial and pretrial publicity on jurors?"[1] There follows a brief summary of theoretical considerations: the tendency of the courts to view the jury trial as a fixed, immutable sanctuary whose mysteries must be forever sacrosanct; the adversary system as a means toward an end as opposed to the unfettered search for truth; the stultifying ritual of precedent as opposed to social change.

This is not to suggest that all members of the legal profession are blind to the value of scientific method in judicial fact-finding or that lawyers conspire to subvert "truth." It does suggest, however, that the conventional logic of the law, with its dependence on analogy, *is an inadequate and naive*

[1] Donald M. Gillmor, "Free Press and Fair Trial: A Continuing Dialogue. Trial by Newspaper and the Social Sciences," *North Dakota Law Review*, 41:156–76 (1965).

74

method when the law reaches out to other disciplines to justify legislation or legal reform. (Emphasis added.)

The author says quite flatly: "[Until the legal profession seeks the counsel of the sociologist and psychologist in solving the pretrial publicity problem] the free press-fair trial conflict will remain simply an issue of passionate speculation."

Chief among the studies cited were the massive Chicago Law School Jury Project, public opinion polls conducted to determine pretrial jury prejudice and content analyses designed to measure the bias of news stories.

Under "current communications research," the author sketched relevant propositions in the study of attitude change and mass communication behavior, concluding: "At the very least, these studies suggest that there is probably no simple and direct cause-effect relationship between pretrial and trial press comment and jury verdicts—although the converse has been held as a law by most Anglo-American courts." Commenting on the evidence as a whole, he says: "If a tentative conclusion may be ventured at this point, it is that there is no empirical evidence to support the view that extensive, or even irresponsible, press coverage of a court case destroys the ability of jurors to decide the issue fairly."

The author concludes by suggesting a massive multi-faceted research program embracing experiments, interviews, content analyses and participant observation.

Goggin and Hanover

Terrance P. Goggin and George M. Hanover[2] set forth the familiar dilemma: "the extent, nature and result of the prejudice created by the news media in the mind of a prospective juror." Following a discussion of the legal concept of an impartial jury, the authors turn to psychological principles for answers to two questions: "First, whether or not a belief in guilt is formed by exposure to incriminating facts; and second, whether or not such a belief prevents a juror from being impartial." The authors cite standard works in social psychology, setting forth the following principles:

---

[2] Terrence P. Goggin and George M. Hanover, "Fair Trial *v.* Free Press: The Psychological Effect of Pre-Trial Publicity on the Juror's Ability to Be Impartial: A Plea for Reform," *Southern California Law Review*, 38:672–88 (1965).

1) People form beliefs, often erroneous, on the basis of a minimum of factual information.

2) People tend to interpret facts, particularly ambiguous facts, in a manner which best satisfies their own needs.

3) People tend to form beliefs in accordance with those of others on the basis of a desire for social acceptance and approval.

4) Beliefs are resistant to change because of unwillingness to alter an original impression as exemplified by the selective nature of perception and memory, which in turn maintains consistency in belief and reenforces misconceptions with more misconceptions in a kind of vicious circle.

5) There is a strong tendency for the vast majority of the public to consider the media reliable, a proposition that becomes especially relevant in the context of an accusation of guilt because the public is quick to form beliefs when a threat against society is perceived and is slow to distinguish between guilt and accusation.

With these propositions as inferential bases, the authors conclude that it is unreasonable to presume impartiality: ". . . it would seem psychologically impossible for a jury to perceive a defendant or anything relating to the defendant, without a belief in the defendant's guilt influencing the perception and reasoning process of the juror."

But to what extent, the authors ask, does such a belief, though not laid aside, affect the juror as a trier of fact? After summarizing once more the psychological principles surrounding belief formation and resistance to change, the authors conclude: "Such a belief can only dramatically intrude upon the juror's analysis of causal relationships and probabilities." The "plea for reform" of the article's title argues for sanctions similar to those contained in the revised Canon 20 of the American Bar Association.

The two reviews, both based on generalizations drawn from the social (behavioral) sciences, arrive at different conclusions. Gillmor finds the results of specific studies inadequate, whereas Goggin and Hanover base their conclusions on generally well supported psychological principles.

At what point may the evidence be interpreted as reasonable proof? And at what point must a proposition be rejected for lack of convincing evidence? These two reviews emphasize the dilemma set forth by Justice Frankfurter. More important, they point up the perils involved in selection, interpretation and emphasis when applying behavioral science research to a specific problem.

The Jury Trial

A TRIAL IS A continuous and cumulative process and hence some risk attaches to treating the successive segments separately. But only by isolating each segment is it possible to confront each with appropriate principles of the behavioral sciences. In addition, in the case of pretrial publicity as it relates to the trial process it is necessary to add a segment—exposure (See Figure 2). While the following discussion treats the segments discretely and one at a time, due allowance must be made for cumulative effects.

Exposure

What happens when a prospective juror is exposed to a news story of a crime? What takes place in terms of attitudes—knowing (cognitive), feeling (affective), and choosing (conative)? How does the prospective juror organize the material? What components of the attitudinal mix are dominant?

One of the most illuminating studies provides convincing evidence that crime stories are organized quite differently within the attitudinal set than other categories of information and that they are heavily identified with the affective components of attitude. Dow set out to test the ability of subjects to "identify" with the criminal offender.[1] The hypothesis was: ". . . the public's attitude toward the offender is a function of the level of identification existing between the two." He defined identification on two dimensions: *empathy*, or imaging oneself in the position of another and *sympathy*, or the capacity to feel sorry for

[1] Thomas E. Dow, Jr., "The Role of Identification in Conditioning Public Attitude Toward the Offender," *The Journal of Criminal Law, Criminology and Police Science*, 58:75–79 (1962).

77

another. Subjects were 549 undergraduates and the variable was the degree of identification, as measured by rank order of empathy and of sympathy for a number of unfortunates (poor, sick, etc.), among them an adult criminal. The conative component of attitude was measured by the subjects' willingness to allot research funds (e.g., to treatment of adult criminals, poor, sick, etc.). In each situation—empathy, sympathy and allocation of research funds—the adult criminal was ranked last. The synopsis of the study concludes: "Their [subjects] ability to [identify] was extremely limited, and provided presumptive evidence that this breakdown in identification had conditioned public attitude toward the offender." In short, the study supports the common sense proposition that the public shuns the criminal.

At this point it is pertinent to ask: What about the distinction between the criminal and the accused? Tans and Chaffee provide evidence that arrest was positively associated with belief in guilt and the Wilcox-McCombs study indicated that a sizable group of prospective jurors could not distinguish between accusation and guilt.[2] There begins to develop, then, a more complex proposition: the criminal is perceived as an undesirable and the distinction between the criminal and the accused is often fuzzy, hence the danger that the innocent will be damned by public opinion before he gets his day in court. Studies and fragments of studies point in the same direction. One such cluster of studies is concerned with the open and the closed mind. The proposition relevant to exposure to a crime story is summarized by Norris:

> One possible index of such a trait is suggested by Rokeach's theoretical general trait of "open-mindedness." He posits that individuals differ in their ability to receive, evaluate and act on information relevant to a particular belief or belief system. Perhaps the major factor determining the degree of open-mindedness, according to Rokeach, is the capacity to distinguish information about a given topic from information about the source of the topic.[3]

Norris tested this proposition in an experiment. Her hypothesis stated that more change could be expected in close-minded subjects in response to the same news stories because the close-minded do not distinguish

[2] Mary Dee Tans and Steven H. Chaffee, "Pretrial Publicity and Juror Prejudice," *Journalism Quarterly*, 43:647–54 (1966); Walter Wilcox and Maxwell McCombs, "Crime Story Elements and Fair Trial/Free Press," unpublished (1967).

[3] Eleanor L. Norris, "Attitude Change as a Function of Open or Closed Mindedness," *Journalism Quarterly*, 42:571–75 (1965).

source from the message. Subjects were 101 undergraduates; the message concerned arguments against four commonly accepted health practices (periodic x-rays, use of penicillin, tooth brushing and medical check-ups); the design was before-after; that is, attitudes toward the health practices were first elicited, the subjects exposed and the amount of change measured. Previously, the subjects had been divided into open-minded (49 subjects) and close-minded (52 subjects) by use of a 40-item scale designed by Rokeach. The hypothesis was confirmed: Relatively closed-minded subjects changed more than those relatively open-minded.

Another cluster of studies centers upon the proposition that initial, albeit minimal, information about a person will be organized into a coherent image, and that there is a tendency to go considerably beyond the initial information to fill out the image. As noted in the report on the Tans and Chaffee study, belief in guilt was correlated with "bad," "dumb" and "dishonest." In short, the filling out of the image consisted largely of adding negative evaluations. Probably the most elaborate behavioral science experiment along these lines was conducted by a team of Harvard social psychologists.[4] The experimenters studied the kinds of inferences involved in forming an overall impression of a personality on the basis of partial or fragmentary information. What kinds of traits are assigned by the subjects as inferred from a single trait? Subjects were 1,320 Boston area college students and the variables were such evaluative terms as intelligent, inconsiderate, etc. The results as reported by the authors:

When the direction or sign [+ or −] of the inferences made from two or three single traits is the same, the inference from their combination is almost universally in the same direction, and the agreement among subjects regarding this direction tends to be greater than in the case of component single traits.

When the two or three traits singly yield inferences of unlike sign, the *sign* of the inference from their combination is determined by the component of which there is more widespread agreement. Under this condition of "conflicting" information, however, the resultant inference does not show

---

[4] Jerome S. Bruner, David Shapiro and Renato Tagiuri, "The Meaning of Traits in Isolation and Combination," in Renato Tagiuri and L. Petrullo, eds., *Person Perception and Interpersonal Behavior* (Stanford: Stanford University Press, 1958), pp. 277–99.

the same relative increase in agreement observed with component inferences of like sign.

For combinations of three traits where the single inferences have unlike signs, the inference from the traits in combination is made in the direction of the dominant sign.

These principles, based on sign and agreement, account for the sign in 97 percent of the inferences made from trait combinations.[5]

The experiment itself is unusually powerful, accounting for 97 percent of variance with a few principles. In establishing the linkage with the crime story, the "signs" might be translated as indicators of guilt or innocence. The central trait might be "arrested" or "convicted criminal" etc. The more negative traits, the greater is the possibility of a negative total image, but when the traits are mixed (arrest, but impeccable background) the total image follows the more powerful of the traits. Kelley, working with student subjects, found that the initial trait ("rather cold" or "very warm") included in the introduction of a person caused significant differences in future evaluations along the dimensions of unsociable, unpopular, irritable, humorless and ruthless, despite the fact that the exposure, a speech by the person in question, was identical.[6] This finding helps explain the Tans/Chaffee finding that arrest itself has a stereotyping effect.

Thus far it has been assumed that a crime story introduces the reader to the accused for the first time. What about a crime story in which the accused is known to the prospective juror, either personally or through reputation? Or a more subtle question: What about a crime story in which the accused is identified with some profession or activity (ministry, gambling) about which the prospective juror could be expected to have a well-defined attitude?

Taking the possibilities one at a time: Annis and Meier hit upon the distinction between initial exposure as opposed to exposure in a familiar context in an early (1934) study, although somewhat inadvertently.[7] In seeking to test whether editorials could affect attitude toward a person, they planted a number of editorials in a student daily newspaper, half of them favorable and half unfavorable to a mythical former prime

[5] *Ibid.*, p. 286.

[6] Harold H. Kelley, "The Warm-Cold Variable in First Impressions of Persons," *Journal of Personality*, 18:431–39 (1950).

[7] Albert D. Annis and Norman C. Meier, "The Introduction of Opinion Through Suggestion by Means of Planted Content," *The Journal of Social Psychology*, 5:65–79 (1934).

minister of Australia. The verdict by 203 student subjects: 98% agreement with the editorials for the favorable variable and 86% agreement for the unfavorable variable. The sleeper in the study was pointed out later in a textbook.[8] The authors held that the opinion was induced *provided that*, instead of *even when*, the person is unknown. The notion that initial impression is uniquely potent is something of a tenet in political communications research. Berelson believes that: "Communication content is more effective in influencing public opinion on new or unconstructed issues, i.e., those not particularly correlated with existing attitude clusters," and it is Hadley Cantril's view that "verbal statements . . . have maximum importance when opinion is unstructured . . ."[9]

The situation becomes somewhat muddled when the accused is known to the prospective juror. Here a complex of interacting factors come into play, illustrated by these polar terms: like/dislike, good/bad, aggressive/retiring, nice/mean, mysterious/simple, etc.; in short, the range of cognitive and affective traits of attitude that make up the evaluation of one person by another. The crime story could be expected to both affect and be affected by these attitudinal traits.

Asch concluded from extensive research with student subjects that 1) there is a tendency to form an impression of a person as a unit based on a central trait, 2) this central trait can vary depending upon the context, 3) two or more impressions tend to combine into the central trait, 4) each trait is a trait of the entire person and the entire person speaks through each of his traits.[10] Applying these propositions to the central trait in question, it may logically be expected that when one trait is involvement in a serious crime, other traits would be reevaluated in light of the crime trait, the degree depending upon the potency of the pretrial publicity as against the potency of the other traits.

The attitudinal variables at work in a situation in which the accused is identified with some prominent profession or activity have been indirectly explored by Rokeach, who holds that an attitude change is a

[8] Gardner Murphy, Lois Barclay Murphy and Theodore M. Newcomb, *Experimental Social Psychology* (New York, Harper & Bros., 1937).

[9] Bernard Berelson, "Communications and Public Opinion," in Wilbur Schramm, ed., *Mass Communications* (Urbana: University of Illinois Press, 1949); Hadley Cantril, "The Use of Trends," in Cantril, ed., *Gauging Public Opinion* (Princeton: Princeton University Press, 1944).

[10] Solomon E. Asch, "Forming Impressions of Personality," *Journal of Abnormal Psychology*, 41:258–90 (1946).

function not merely of attitudes toward objects but attitudes toward situations.[11] By extension of this principle, the context of the situation may be expected to have some effect on the attitude toward a person. The linkage to the trial process is highly tenuous, but sufficient to pose the question: Does the prospective juror react differently in terms of guilt or innocence for an accused with high prestige (e.g., doctor) than for an accused with low prestige (e.g., prostitute) with the nature of the crime held constant? An experiment in a quite separate context (belief that people should have a right of reply to an article in a newspaper) indicates that people are indeed able to sort the salient issue from the context of the situation.[12] In this study respondents were asked whether the person (e.g., mayor of a city) described in a case situation should have the legal right of reply to a specific newspaper article (e.g., poor judgment in garbage removal policy). They were also asked their opinions of the persons in a general context (e.g., city political leader). In each of ten such cases, respondents quite clearly kept the issue distinct from the context.

Recasting the question: Does the reporting of the occupation, background and reputation of an accused person have a measurable effect on the prospective juror's perception of his guilt or innocence? What little evidence exists indicates that the ability to sort out the issue from the background is present in some degree for prospective jurors. Further, given the assumption that accusation of a crime creates a powerful central trait for the accused, the question of contextual setting in terms of occupation, background and reputation may well be irrelevant.

Walter Lippman wrote—years ago—that:

For the most part we do not first see, and then define, we define first and then see. In the great blooming, buzzing confusion of the outer world we pick out what our culture has already defined for us, and we tend to perceive that which we have picked out in the form stereotyped for us by our culture.[13]

Does the summoned venireman bring bias with him to the court house? How much of it is attributable to the press? On balance, the evidence cited above points consistently toward a degree of bias toward

[11] Milton Rokeach, "Attitude Change and Behavioral Change," *Public Opinion Quarterly*, 30:529–50 (1966–67).

[12] Walter Wilcox, "Right of Reply in the United States," *Gazette*, 34:1–6 (1968).

[13] Walter Lippmann, *Public Opinion* (New York: Macmillan, 1924), p. 81.

guilt. But it also points with equal persistence that the roots of the bias lie deeper than press reports—in the alienation of the accused, in the hasty formation of an image based on a fragment of information, on the inability of some to distinguish between accusation and guilt; in short, on the highly complex way in which people absorb and evaluate information irrespective of how they acquire such information.

Jury Selection: Venire

Veniremen are typically empanelled in numbers three or more times that required for the jury itself. The setting is official, the mien of the court stern, the task solemn: yesterday a small businessman or housewife, today a citizen. The literature of the law abounds in discussion of the jury system, revolving around such matters as composition as it reflects the population, competence in evaluating evidence, ability to grasp the law, etc.—in short, the efficacy of the jury system. These problems are not at issue here except as they pertain to behavioral science research that illuminates the social-psychological change that may occur when a citizen is empanelled for jury duty. Does he indeed change? In what way? More specifically, is it logical to assume that his role as a venireman will affect the way in which he evaluates previous information about the crime and the accused?

It should be emphasized that at this point the panel is not a group but a collection of individuals playing individual roles; later, the jurors will coalesce into a group, at which point small group research becomes relevant.

The first and obvious question is: What effect does the time lag between exposure to pretrial publicity and empanelling the venire have upon its retention? Learning and forgetting is a phenomenon familiar to every school child. The principles are: 1) the better material is learned the less likely it will be forgotten, 2) the more often the learner is reminded, or reenforced, the less likely he will forget, and 3) forgetting takes place rapidly at first and then levels off.[14] In applying these principles to the effects of exposure, it makes sense to say that the more potent the pretrial publicity the longer it will be remembered and, conversely, the less potent the more quickly it will be forgotten, provided one or more reminders do not refresh and continuously re-constitute the

---

[14] Bernard Berelson and Gary A. Steiner, *Human Behavior* (New York: Harcourt Brace and World, 1964), pp. 133–237.

memory. The celebrated crime case, with massive and continuous pre-trial publicity, can logically be expected to persist in the memory longer than that of a routine case with no intervening stories. These common sense assumptions are straight-forward and really need no confirmation. However, a complicating factor is found in the notions of "proactive inhibition" and "retroactive inhibition." Berelson and Steiner describe them essentially as follows:[15]

Cast in terms of the principle that if the interval between learning and the test for retention is held constant and if the material is learned at the same level of proficiency for each condition, then:

1) A person who learns about a body of material and is not exposed to similar materials should have the best recall of the material.

2) A person who learns about a body of material but who has been exposed to similar material previously should have the next best recall (proactive inhibition).

3) A person who learns about a body of material and then later is ex-posed to similar material should have the least recall of the original material (retroactive inhibition).

Further, the more similar the materials the more pronounced the inhibiting effects. This impinges on a notion called "negative transfer" which holds that people tend to transfer knowledge about one set of materials to another similar set, and the closer the similarity the greater the tendency.

This would mean that the venireman should have the *greatest* mem-ory for publicity when he is not exposed to any other crime stories before or after, should have *less* capacity when the pretrial publicity is preceded by other crime stories, should have the *least* capacity when other crime stories follow the pretrial publicity, and the more similar the crime stories the greater the loss of ability to recall the one in question.

Frederic C. Bartlett developed insights into still another memory phenomenon.[16] A sturdy survivor since 1932, his view holds that people tend to condense or crystallize the central characteristic of a message while forgetting the details. Later, when called upon to reconstruct the message, they react according to their personalities, some adding detail in wild profusion and others only parsimoniously, neither with any ac-curacy. This would mean in the trial jury context that attempts to re-

[15] *Ibid.*, p. 164.

[16] Frederic C. Bartlett, *Remembering* (Cambridge: Cambridge University Press, 1932), p. 22.

store the details of a crime story may be either unsuccessful, ("I don't remember the details but . . .") or highly inaccurate, (getting the crime story mixed up with other information, impressions and fancy). This principle receives additional support from the notion of negative transfer, discussed under retroactive inhibition above.

Bartlett contributed still another principle—that of social factors in recall.[17] In brief, this notion holds that each person remembers best that material which is familiar, relevant and important to his life. By extension, veniremen bring with them as many different memory frameworks as there are veniremen: a bricklayer might recall vividly that the accused is a bricklayer but remember little else, a mother that the accused has children, etc.

But probably the most powerful factor in remembering and forgetting is based on a common-sense interpretation of the foregoing behavioral principles: people forget; perhaps the venireman has simply forgotten entirely or the event has grown dim in the face of the myriad other messages that have emerged to compete for a place in active memory.

Other more subtle dimensions of time lag have been explored, mostly in a cluster of studies performed by Carl Hovland, his associates and his successors. Insko has summarized these findings.[18]

Source credibility. The effect upon attitude is initially greater when it comes from a high credibility source than a low credibility source. However, the source effect disappears after a time or "decays;" that is, the source of the message disintegrates in the memory of the subjects; further, there is evidence that the effect is due to a tendency to dissociate source and content and not simply to forget the source. While these findings are hedged with untested variables (e.g., whether the source was "trustworthy" or "expert") the central proposition points in a single direction: people tend to remember the message while forgetting the connection to the source. This would mean in the present context, that some loss of attribution ("police said," etc.) may logically be expected in the course of the forgetting process, and consequently the ability to distinguish between guilt and accusation, already rather shaky for many prospective jurors, may be further eroded as the attitudinal set toward the event dims. But this notion is complicated by the "sleeper effect," an increase in opinion change over a period of time after receiving a mes-

[17] *Ibid.*, summarized, p. 267.

[18] Chester A. Insko, *Theories of Attitude Change* (New York: Appleton-Century-Crofts, 1967), pp. 12–63.

sage from a low credibility source. Hovland and Weiss offer evidence that people do not necessarily associate source and message after the passage of time.[19] Also, Kelman and Hovland found that the "reinstatement" of the source, or linking source and message once more, had the effect of restoring the original relationships with respect to high and low source credibility.[20]

These experiments suggest that in empanelling a venire, memory of the link between the crime and the accused has been reinstated by the very act of empanellment.

Inoculation. A phenomenon called "inoculation" is relevant here, although the data must be recast and redirected to make them applicable. The theory, as set forth by McGuire, holds in part that ". . . pretreatments designed to make truisms resistant to subsequent persuasive attacks will be effective to the extent they overcome two basic difficulties: one, the believer is unpracticed in defending his belief; and two, he is unmotivated to undertake the necessary practice."[21] In a series of experiments McGuire found that he could create a certain immunity against persuasion by attacking truisms under a series of communication conditions. The cultural truisms of the experiments were health beliefs such as "it's a good idea to brush your teeth after each meal if possible." Subjects were college students. Manipulation consisted of a variety of message conditions, e.g., warning that an attack upon the truism was forthcoming. McGuire warns that the experiments dealt in truisms only and not in controversial beliefs, and that application of inoculation theory to controversial situations is not warranted. Application to the jury trial, then, must be carefully qualified.

Scars, Freedman and O'Connor used simulated juries composed of students to test the effects of anticipated debate on the polarization of opinion.[22] The exposure included opening statements, testimony and

[19] Carl I. Hovland and Walter Weiss, "The Influence of Source Credibility on Communication Effectiveness," *Public Opinion Quarterly,* 15: 635–50 (1951).

[20] Herbert C. Kelman and Carl I. Hovland, " 'Reinstatement' of the Communicator in Delayed Measurement of Opinion Change," *Journal of Abnormal and Social Psychology,* 48:327–35 (1953).

[21] William J. McGuire, "Inducing Resistance to Persuasion," in Leonard Berkowitz, ed., *Advances in Experimental Psychology,* Vol. 1 (New York: Academic Press, 1964), pp. 191–229.

[22] David O. Sears, Jonathan L. Freedman and Edward F. O'Connor, Jr., "The Effects of Anticipated Debate and Commitment on the Polarization of Audience Opinion," *Public Opinion Quarterly,* 28:615–27 (1964).

summation, and the pertinent variable was whether debate was to take place. Subjects were asked to declare the degree of certainty with respect to opinions of guilt or innocence. The authors concluded that anticipating a debate "polarized" the opinions of those with a high degree of certainty. Or, stated another way, those confident of their decisions were more likely to build resistance to a forthcoming debate and those lacking confidence were inclined to return to a neutral position in preparation for the debate.

Freedman and Sears probed still another dimension—that warning of a communication hostile to an attitude builds resistance to change.[23] Subjects were high school students; the message concerned: "Why Teen-Agers Should Not Drive." Those warned resisted change in response to a speech to a significantly higher degree than those not warned. In the venire situation, the veniremen are indeed warned that an attempt will be made to change attitudes. Hence, the inference here is that resistance will accrue according to the attitudinal set the venireman brings to the courtroom respecting the guilt or innocence of the accused.

In sum, the studies presented in this section point to the possibility that veniremen crystallize and consolidate the cognitive and affective ingredients of the attitudinal set in anticipation of the trial. But to what degree, in what direction and with what measurable effect the evidence is not clear.

Jury Selection: Voir Dire

The *voire dire* examination is an open-court proceeding in which attorneys for both sides examine prospective jurors, challenge jurors for cause and (usually) exercise the right to make a fixed number of peremptory challenges. Among the causes for such challenge is, of course, any indication that the venireman has made up his mind about guilt or innocence or gives evidence of being prejudiced for any reason, including exposure to pretrial publicity.

The essential question, then, is: How effective is *voir dire* in screening from the jury those veniremen who have formed opinions based on pretrial publicity? In the present context this question resolves into two

[23] Jonathan L. Freedman and David O. Sears, "Warning, Distraction and Resistance to Influence," *Journal of Personality and Social Psychology*, 2:262–66 (1965).

sub-questions: 1) Can *voir dire* neutralize the manifest cognitive and affective gestalt acquired through pretrial publicity? 2) What are the effects of the *voir dire* process upon the way the juror organizes pretrial information?

Dale W. Broeder, a staff member of the University of Chicago Jury Project, casts some doubts on the efficacy of *voire dire*.[24] Broader conducted exhaustive interviews with 225 jurors and most of the lawyers involved in 23 consecutive trials before a federal district court in the Midwest. After pointing out the limitations of the sample and posting a warning that no generalizations should be drawn, Broader set forth the following points as "evident:"

1) *Voir dire* is grossly ineffective as a screening mechanism; 2) Many of the reasons for its ineffectiveness are independent of the particular cases studied and of the court in which they were tried; 3) Jurors often, either consciously or unconsciously, lie on *voir dire*; 4) *Voir dire* is utilized much more effectively as a forum for indoctrination than as a means of sifting out potentially unfavorable jurors; and 5) Jurors prefer that the "open court" *voir dire* be retained rather than abolished in favor of some kind of *in camera* proceeding.

These points must be treated as untested propositions. However, Broeder's findings are rather convincing. Perhaps *voir dire* is not sufficiently powerful to screen out strong cognitive and affective imprints and it would be naive to assume that it serves to cleanse the mind of facts or that it can eliminate prejudiced jurors.

The more subtle question of the way in which the juror organizes pretrial publicity in the context of his new role pertains to commitment. The assumption is that a juror has made a public commitment when he denies under questioning that foreknowledge will affect his judgment, or, stated another way, that he will consider no evidence not presented at the trial. This public commitment may cast the juror into three roles: 1) as a citizen serving in a public capacity, 2) as an incipient member of a small group, the values and norms of which he must observe if the group is to accomplish its task and 3) as an amateur under the surveillance of a highly authoritative expert—the trial judge. The behavioral science research bearing on individual reaction to these roles is volumi-

[24] Dale W. Broeder, "Voir Dire Examinations: An Empirical Study," *Southern California Law Review*, 38:503–28 (1965).

nous but peripheral.[25] Sears, Freedman and O'Connor summarized it by saying that "manipulating commitment to the publicness of . . . endorsement . . . has been shown to make the opinion more resistant to change."[26]

On balance, it is speculative but nevertheless reasonable to assume that *voir dire* probably has little effect on the cognitive effects of pretrial publicity concerning previous criminal record or confession, but that it does have some effect on the total attitudinal set of the juror in that it forces him to reorganize the relevant information in the light of this new role, the chief impact being upon the affective component of attitude. This in turn must be tempered by the potency and nature of the pretrial publicity itself: Celebrated case or routine case? Sensational coverage or low key coverage? Notorious personality or unknown person? In short, what odds does the juror face in adapting to his new role? At some risk, it may be suggested that the more potent the pretrial publicity the less potent the commitment in the context of *voir dire*.

Physical Appearances

The juror confronts the accused physically. Previously, in the discussion of exposure, it was shown that people tend to form a coherent image from a fragment of information. Allport concludes that one person's perception of another is heavily conditioned by his attitudinal set (prejudices).[27] Kalven and Zeisel, in the main jury project report, found time and again that appearance, age, family situation, race, health, sex and even matters such as military service had a pronounced effect on the jury's sympathy or hostility.[28] Some comments by judges responding to the Chicago Jury Project questionnaire illustrate the phenomenon in action:

"Defendant came into court on crutches. He was a crippled polio victim. He cried on the stand and obtained the jury's sympathy" (p. 203). "Tenant farmer—elderly. No criminal record, honest, hard worker" (p. 200).

[25] Edward E. Jones and Harold B. Gerard, *Foundations of Social Psychology* (New York: John Wiley, 1967), pp. 309–430.

[26] *Op. cit.*

[27] Gordon W. Allport, *The Nature of Prejudice* (Garden City: Doubleday, 1958).

[28] Harry Kalven, Jr., and Hans Zeisel, *The American Jury* (Boston: Little, Brown, 1966), pp. 193–218.

"Youth and ignorance" (p. 203).

". . . was 1) an attractive woman 2) claimed she had TB and wore a white mask throughout the trial 3) she had a loyal husband who was well liked 4) mother of a fine 12-year-old boy 5) she provided for her mother" (p. 201).

"Boy's mother present. She was old and looked poor" (p. 204).

"Defendant was enlisted in Navy. Subsequent conversation revealed that the jury did not wish to see defendant's record spoiled" (p. 207).

"The defendant [a Negro] did not take the stand but because of his association with the white victims and because of the loss of sight in one eye, he may have made a bad impression on the jury" (p. 383).

"The defendant gave the picture of a pious old fraud. She took her seat in plain view of the jury with a big cross swinging from her neck and thereupon opened her bible in front of her. Then she brought out a bottle of smelling salts, preparing herself spiritually and mentally for any eventuality" (p. 383).

"Defendant did not make a good impression. He was insolent-looking and smart" (p. 383).

The initial gestalt is now being subjected to substantial forces for change. The confrontation builds upon the gestalt, and can logically be expected to have one of four effects upon the impression acquired from pretrial publicity: 1) modify hostility, 2) modify sympathy, 3) enhance hostility and 4) enhance sympathy. (A fifth possibility—no change—may be considered remote; if it exists at all, it is perhaps due to an accident of probability or of two impressions cancelling each other out.) Again, the effect is chiefly in the affective component of attitude ("Could this mild little man possibly commit such a crime?") as opposed to the cognitive component ("He is deceptively mild, considering his long criminal record").

The confrontation, then, must be considered as another item in the attitudinal mix that builds upon the pretrial gestalt and will be in turn develop further as the trial progresses.

Trial Arguments

The body of theory and research focusing upon the effects of persuasive argument is massive indeed. The task of relating it to the highly stylized and rigidly proscribed system of argument in a jury trial is difficult. The problem is further complicated by the fact that the relevant research is heavy on theory but light on convincing experimental evidence.

One-sided and two-sided messages: The jury trial presumably guarantees a two-sided presentation. The assumption is that of a self righting mechanism.

McGuire has demonstrated that if the prior messages are largely one-sided and combined with weak counter messages, subsequent two-sided communications are likely to be perceived in terms of the earlier experience.[29] This fits the pattern of pretrial publicity in many cases and hence the trial arguments might be perceived in the context of some distortion created by pretrial bias.

Primacy vs. Recency: Which is more potent, the first exposure to a message (primacy), in this case pretrial publicity, or the last exposure (recency), in this case trial testimony? Considerable research has focused upon this question with equivocal and uneven results. Rosnow, in an article aptly titled "Whatever Happened to the Law of Primacy," reviews the research and assigns certain kinds of messages to categories.[30] He finds that primacy is the most potent in order of presentation for a controversial topic, a familiar topic and interesting subject matter; recency is the most potent for the non-controversial, unfamiliar and uninteresting. If this is correct, for two of the three message categories relevant to pretrial publicity two are ruled by primacy and one by recency (unfamiliar topic). But Rosnow says a third category—strong argument—over-power primacy and recency. Thus the fact that pretrial publicity is associated with primacy is immaterial wherever strong argument is effective.

Admonition

In his instructions, the judge admonishes the jurors not to consider any matters other than the evidence presented in court. Failure to give such instruction has been held reversible error and appellate courts generally assume such instructions are obeyed. But are they in practice? Doubts center around the following assertions: 1) Such instructions cannot "brainwash" jurors. 2) Jurors may simply disregard them. 3) They may, instead, refresh the jurors' memory of the inadmissible material.[31]

[29] *Op. cit.*

[30] R. L. Rosnow, "Whatever Happened to the Law of Primacy," *Journal of Communication*, 16:10–31 (1966).

[31] Carolyn Jaffee, "The Press and the Oppressed—A Study of Prejudicial Reporting in Criminal Cases," *The Journal of Criminal Law, Criminology and Police Service*, 56:1–17 (1965).

Four questions are at issue here. Two are pragmatic: Does pretrial publicity emerge openly in the jury deliberations? Do instructions have sufficient power to prevent one or more jurors from passing along items of pretrial publicity to the others? The other two are more subtle: Can the juror indeed marshall the mental discipline necessary to deliberately "forget" pretrial publicity? Further, even if he resolutely sets it aside, might it not have a subconscious effect?

Research bearing upon these questions is sparse. Kline and Jess furnished a wisp of evidence that jurors take instructions seriously.[32] In one trial deliberation, a mock juror mentioned a previous criminal record, a pretrial publicity item not in evidence. The transcript shows that after a brief debate the jury agreed that ". . . we're not supposed to take this into consideration now . . . past action isn't supposed to have a bearing on what we're deciding now." Harry Kalven, Jr., of the Chicago Jury Project, wrote: "We do . . . have evidence that the jurors take with surprising seriousness the admonition not to read the paper or to discuss the case with other people. . . ."[33] It seems reasonable that the jurors would respond in like manner to instructions not to discuss pretrial matters. In any event, there is too little evidence on which to base an answer to the first two questions posed above. It would appear to be a promising area for further research.

Answers to the second two questions, if such answers exist, reside somewhere in the notions set forth in the previous section. It might be hypothesized that the judge's instructions interpose a dominating variable, as does the power of argument. They have the advantage of recency and of high credibility and they can logically be expected to have their fear arousing aspects. But these concepts, alone or together, fail to resolve the doubts set forth at the outset of this section. Previously, it was proposed that a cognitive element of pretrial publicity such as previous criminal record, if unchallenged, would pass through the argument stage intact, although its relative position in the total mix of messages might be altered. The judge's instructions attack this message in an indirect way in that the jury is told to set aside any such messages, although typically the message in question is not identified specifically. But confounding the issue is the problem mentioned above: the instruc-

[32] F. Gerald Kline and Paul H. Jess, "Prejudicial Publicity: Its Effects on Law School Mock Juries," *Journalism Quarterly*, 43:113–16 (1966).

[33] Quoted in Donald Gillmor, "Free Press and Fair Trial: A Continuing Dialogue—Trial by Newspaper and the Social Sciences," *North Dakota Law Review*, 41:156–76 (1965).

tions may refresh the juror's memory about extraneous information and reinforce its original effect.

In sum, then, it may fairly be said that the judge's admonition can have a pronounced effect on the control of extra-trial information—and it may not. More evidence is needed on this point.

Deliberation

When the jury retires to deliberate, the process of transformation from twelve individuals into a cohesive small group is sharply accelerated. Interaction, or face-to-face confrontation and communication, triggers a whole new cluster of phenomena. And here the focus of the relevant behavioral science findings shifts from emphasis upon the individual to emphasis upon the group. Volumes have been published about consensus and communication in small groups, including reports of many group decision experiments.[34] The relevant research here is confined to "the problem-solving group, e.g., a committee with a task to perform."[35]

The small group strongly influences the behavior of its members by setting and/or enforcing standards (norms) for proper behavior by its members...[36]

One of the mock jurors in the Kline/Jess experiment said when previous criminal record crept into the discussion: "All right knock that from the record," evidently responding to group pressures.[37] But it would be a mistake to assume the group sanction is in the direction of the judge's admonition. A group norm could form around the value, "all right let's get this over with," or some other value.

Group sanctions are strong. As Berelson and Steiner say in summarizing them:

The response of the group to deviation from its norms for behavior is, first, discussion and persuasion to bring the dissenting minority into line; second, disapproval of the dissenters; third, lowered ranking for the dissenters; fourth, their expulsion or induced resignation from the group.[38]

[34] Edward E. Jones and Harold B. Gerard, *Foundations of Social Psychology* (New York: John Wiley, 1967), pp. 331–86.

[35] *Op. cit.*, p. 326.

[36] *Ibid.*, p. 321.

[37] *Op. cit.*

[38] *Op. cit.*, p. 337.

The powerful urge to conform in the small group setting has been demonstrated repeatedly in experimental situations. Most frequently cited is a study by Asch.[39] The hypothesis was that a person will yield to the group norm even when sense data tell him otherwise. The subjects, 123 undergraduates, were brought into a room in groups of 7 to 9 and asked in sequence to select from among three display lines of varying length the one that was nearest in length to a standard line, a simple task that produced no errors in pretesting. But all but the last subject were "stooges" who deliberately picked the wrong line. The last man yielded to the consensus of his peers—against clear visual evidence—with remarkable frequency. Only one in four resisted completely and on the average subjects made between four and five errors out of a possible 12. This result has been obtained in a number of subsequent studies. The Asch study, while a classic in the sense it has opened new vistas for research, may tend to over-simplify the conformity phenomenon. Asch himself and others have explored a number of variables, including anonymity, ambiguity, number of alternatives, degree of interdependence among group members and a change in attitudinal structure to achieve balance.[40] Such studies have one trait in common: consensus-seeking in small groups such as a jury is a process of yielding to the power of numbers. As Berelson and Steiner put it: "The deviant members of the group are more likely to change their behavior to meet the standards of the modal members of the group than the other way around,"[41] and ". . . a single individual tends not to hold out against the weight of an otherwise unanimous group judgment, even on matters in which the group is clearly in error."[42]

What are the implications here for the problem at hand? The linkage is rather firm and leads to the following proposition: pretrial publicity messages tend to be absorbed, or modified or diminished in the consensus if the modal group is playing its expected role in ignoring such publicity; however, if the consensus builds around the pretrial publicity itself, the opposite effect must be expected.

What if the group leader—either manifest as the jury foreman or latent as a juror with a potent personality—possesses pretrial information that the other jurors do not? Would his attempts to persuade tend

[39] Op. cit.
[40] Jones and Gerard, op. cit., pp. 387–430.
[41] Op. cit., p. 332.
[42] Ibid., p. 335.

to succeed? Experimental literature is not sufficiently on point for a strong inference but it suggests that leaders tend to conform.[43]

Strodtbeck, James and Hawkins, working on one facet of the Chicago Jury Project, found that the juror of high occupational status on a scale of business proprietor/clerical worker/skilled worker/laborer is more likely to be foreman and participates more in the deliberation.[44]

In the jury room, pretrial publicity, an example of "mass" communication, makes a direct confrontation with jury deliberation, an example of interpersonal communication. The work of Paul Lazarsfeld and his associates at Columbia University would appear to be pertinent here.[45] Although they expected to find that the media had massive effects on voters in an election campaign, they found significant influence was exerted by personal associates. Successive studies of other elections, consumer preferences and the adoption of new drugs by physicians convinced them that interpersonal influence is more effective than mass media influence.

This generalization has been one of the most frequently asserted and widely attacked in behavioral science. Both Pool and Lang and Lang have shown that the data upon which it is based do not lead to the conclusions drawn by the Columbia group.[46] More recent work has tended to emphasize the interplay of mass media and interpersonal influences, rather than treating them as competitors.

At this stage of the trial the juror has been exposed to hundreds, even thousands, of messages—important and trivial, contradictory and complementary, consonant and dissonant; it is a microcosm of Lippmann's "great, blooming, buzzing confusion." As the mental effort to maintain each message separately becomes overwhelming, the juror must reduce

[43] Berelson and Steiner, pp. 341–46.

[44] Fred M. Strodtbeck, Rita M. James and Charles Hawkins, "Social Status in Jury Deliberations," *American Sociological Review* 22:713–19 (1957).

[45] Paul Lazarsfeld, Bernard Berelson and Hazel Gaudet, *The People's Choice* (New York: Columbia University Press, 1948); Bernard Berelson, Paul F. Lazarsfeld and William N. McPhee, *Voting* (Chicago: University of Chicago Press, 1954); Elihu Katz and Paul F. Lazarsfeld, *Personal Influence* (Glencoe, Ill.: Free Press, 1955); Herbert Menzel and Elihu Katz, "Social Relations and Innovation in the Medical Profession," *Public Opinion Quarterly*, 19:337–52 (1955).

[46] Ithiel deSola Pool, "TV: A New Dimension in Politics," in E. Burdick and A. J. Brodbeck, eds., *American Voting Behavior* (Glencoe, Ill.: Free Press, 1959), pp. 197–208; Kurt Lang and Gladys E. Lang, "The Mass Media and Voting," in Burdick and Brodbeck, *ibid.*, pp. 217–35.

this massive intake into a cohesive gestalt. The group norm provides him with a standard against which he can examine, evaluate, accept, reject and, ultimately, anchor his gestalt. Hence, the small group is not only a mediating unit for conformity, but a sanctuary for the resolution of many messages into one cohesive message.

The question is: how does pretrial publicity fare in the face of group conformity behavior? It is clear that group processes tend to produce a consensus among interacting groups. Would this necessarily be on the side of justice, fair play and the judge's admonition? If the judge's admonition succeeds in producing a modal position that is against consideration of information not given in evidence, it could be expected that the group would coalesce around that position, as appeared to be the case in the mock trials of Kline and Jess. In that case the juror who injects pretrial publicity into the deliberations may expect to conform or be rejected by the group. But consensus may as readily develop around the shared (modal) view that the defendant must be guilty because he's had so many prior convictions.

Verdict

The conative or "choosing" ingredient of behavior has been subjected to numerous experiments, most of them based on free choice of minor alternatives; e.g., to buy baby food or to show up for an experiment.[47] Typically, the conative ingredient of the attitudinal mix is minimized in the before/after experiment, as the experimenter cannot reasonably expect a highly significant act from a casual experimental subject. It makes methodological sense for such research to begin with the act itself and probe backward for behavioral and demographic patterns.

A major study of the trial jury provides a rich harvest of the decision behavior of juries.[48] In this work, Harry Kalven, Jr., and Hans Zeisel of the Chicago Jury Project explored the workings of the American trial jury. The problem was: what factors affect the jury in arriving at a verdict in a criminal trial? The sample was 3,576 jury trials reported by 555 trial judges in the United States. Mailed questionnaires reported on trials held during two periods, 1954–55 and 1958, with some overlap into adjacent years. The method was to compare the jury verdicts with the judgment of the trial judge in each case in a search

---

[47] Jones and Gerard, op. cit., pp. 331–86.
[48] Kalven and Zeisel, op. cit.

for insights into the variables that affect verdicts. The variables included the nature of the evidence and its credibility, sentiments about the defendant, self-defense, degree of punishment, impact of the lawyer, type of case and others. The study did not search for effects of pretrial publicity. "As a matter of prudence we decided not to interview in major criminal cases where there was trial by newspaper."[49] But the proposition that knowledge of previous criminal record is a potent factor in jury verdicts was subsequently confirmed in an interview with Professor Kalven.[50]

In discussing cases in which the judge disagreed with the jury, the authors devote a section to "Facts Only the Judge Knew."[51] This resulted in a rather curious twist of prejudicial pretrial publicity. The judge in some cases would convict whereas the jury acquits. In one case, the judge reported: "The jury did not know that she, a young woman accused of being accomplice to armed robbery, had a record of murder with parole from a manslaughter conviction."[52] In another: "Jury did not realize as I did from past experience with defendant that he was a dangerous man when drinking."[53] And: "In one case the jury acquits a mother of several children of the charge of defrauding a finance company by selling mortgaged property. The judge, in disagreeing, notes that he alone knew that she had 'previously been charged with the same crime and had been acquitted'."[54]

The judges are assuming that if the jurors had known about the defendants' criminal records the verdict would have been guilty. More directly, the study cites statistical evidence that the defendant who has a record and who does not take the stand is at a disadvantage when compared with the defendant who does not have a record and who does take the stand. This, the authors believe, ". . . lends support to the legal tradition which closely guards the disclosure of a prior record in a criminal case."[55] The authors cite as a typical comment: "Jury knew the defendant's bad record."

In another section the study reports that in 13 percent of the cases

---

[49] Quoted in Gillmor, *op. cit.*
[50] Interview with the author May 2, 1968.
[51] Kalven and Zeisel, *op. cit.*, p. 122.
[52] *Loc. cit.*
[53] P. 123.
[54] P. 126.
[55] P. 389.

(156 trials) involving defendants with previous criminal records, the jury learned of the record.[56] Jurors were exposed to the information for a "variety of reasons," among them but not necessarily the most prevalent: ". . . its sheer notoriety may obviate any attempt at concealment."[57] In still another section the researchers found another bit of evidence that the criminal record is a potent factor.

In a homicide case, the judge finds the death accidental, whereas the jury convicts of involuntary manslaughter. The distinctive circumstance is that the jury somehow, from sources outside of the trial, knows of the defendant's repute and even that he has criminal record, whereas the judge does not learn of these matters until after the verdict is in. As the judge puts it by way of explanation: "The defendant was not well thought of locally and that fact was known to the jury but not by the judge until after the verdict."[58]

The obvious conclusion to be drawn from these data is that a single pretrial cognitive element—criminal record—tended to have an effect. Apparently, knowledge of the record can indeed survive from exposure to verdict.

Nowhere in the Kalven and Zeisel data is there clear evidence that affective pretrial elements have a measurable effect. Throughout, with the exception on criminal record, the data, in particular the judges' comments, concern the attitudinal mix developed *during the trial* and not before the trial. This should not be interpreted to mean there were no pretrial attitudinal biases; the study did not probe this question. But such a bias did not emerge as a matter of chance as did criminal record.

The confession is touched upon only fleetingly:

Two young boys, charged with burglary, make a sympathetic appearance before the jury. The judge not only knows something deprivational about the boys' reputations but also tells us that "one of the defendants offered to plead guilty [confess] but the other insisted on taking his chances with the jury. As a result both were acquitted."[59]

The researchers were unable to establish firmly the effects of a repudiated confession. In only .6 per cent of 146 close cases of serious

[56] P. 147.
[57] *Loc. cit.*
[58] P. 391.
[59] P. 125.

crime did the judge disagree with the jury and among these nine cases the jury acquitted, whereas the judge would have convicted.[60]

The Kalven and Zeisel data indicate that of 1,191 cases, in 5 percent the evidence was clear for acquittal, in 43 percent the evidence was close and in 52 percent it was clear for conviction.[61] In all cases competing messages may be thought of as continuously cancelling each other out. But in the close case the jury must reach a verdict on the basis of a minimal message that barely tips the balance. The temptation for the jury to seek out, to revive, to reassess pretrial information in an effort to resolve a close case may be appreciably greater than for a clear case. The relevant behavioral science research model would: 1) create a balanced set of cancelling messages, 2) observe the degree to which subjects seek additional messages, and 3) evaluate the kinds and pertinence of these messages. As no such experiment has been attempted, the notion must join the list of untested propositions.

[60] P. 174.
[61] P. 135.

Conclusions

If one counts himself a member of the anything-is-possible school of behavioral research and, additionally, is at home with the most sophisticated computer technology, he might conceive a mathematical model through which to apply behavioral science concepts to the three-way riddle of pretrial publicity/jury trial/behavioral science.

First, it would be necessary to scale the various concepts; for example, placing variables such as open/closed mind, routine/celebrated trial on 7-point scales, and so on through the entire range of variables, to which would be added all possible combinations of jury trial situations. And finally the data would be analyzed for interactions to determine the relative influence or loading that each variable brings to each verdict. The notion is, of course, fantastic; it is set forth here to emphasize a central point: presently existing behavioral science theories, principles, concepts, postulates and experiments, by themselves or in limited combinations, cannot be expected to yield definitive explanations.

Of the various propositions set forth only one—the potency of the previous criminal record—seems to persist throughout. It received support from both the empirical evidence in the Kalven and Zeisel study and the Tans and Chaffee study from behavioral science research. But the implication seems clear: the temptation to quote from the behavioral sciences in support of the effects of pretrial publicity one way or the other, must be disciplined by perspective. Their tenuous linkage to the jury trial combine to give a low yield in terms of direct application. This is not to say that the evidence so provided need be ignored; rather it must be properly assigned to its niche in terms of the total evidence. Further, when quoted without its supporting cast of mediating variables and outside the social science context, it tends to become an indigestible lump of information, without meaning. But to ignore the lessons of the behavioral science because of their tenuous linkage to the jury trial or because of the difficulty in establishing prudent perspective would be to yield to the opposite temptation—the easy way out by another door.

Much of the difficulty in establishing the necessary exposure/trial/ research linkage is not attributable to the power of the behavioral sciences themselves but to the fact that they have not been oriented to the uniqueness of the jury trial system. In other fields (marketing, learning, propaganda) they are on point and they figure significantly in day-to-day decisions. Hence, their comparatively low efficacy here must be considered one of application and not one of inherent limitation.

Not that the behavioral sciences, refocused and brought to bear upon the problem, will automatically root out all the answers. Schur points out the pitfalls when "rule-logicians . . . seek to reduce law and legal process to some sort of dehumanized objectivity." But, Schur concludes:

> To recognize that the judicial process may fall largely within the realm of the ideographic rather than that of the nomothetic, that the reality of criminal law is social reality irreducible to dehumanized objectivity, is not cause for extreme pessimism. Rather, such recognition serves to put studies of criminal justice in their proper methodological perspective, to emphasize the value of studying the underlying human purposes and meanings attached to the action under study, and to stress the importance of investigator's purpose at hand in shaping the type of analysis that will be most fruitful. While we must acknowledge severe obstacles to achieving a truly empirical legal "science," the very acceptance of such limitations may pave the way for increased understanding of the process of criminal justice as a segment of human action in the social world.[1]

In fact, if and when the behavioral science techniques are brought to bear directly and on point the results in illuminating the question posed at the outset of this review could be quite dramatic.

From the viewpoint of immediate utility, all signs seem to point to the criminal record as a potent pretrial publicity element. This in itself is no new finding. But its linkage to pretrial publicity is not complete. The implication as to whether jurors learn of the record through the press, or at the trial or through common knowledge has not been sorted

---

[1] Edwin M. Schur, "Scientific Method and the Criminal Trial Decision," *Social Research*, 25:173–90 (1958).

out. Nor does there seem any feasible way of keeping a criminal record secret.

What happened to the confession, a prime suspect in the Wilcox/ McCombs study? It simply did not emerge in the Kalven/Zeisel study to other than an offhand and negligible extent, nor did any behavioral science study cluster shed any illumination. And the other elements in the pretrial publicity configuration? They, too, must remain in the realm of speculation.

As pretrial publicity was traced through the jury trial, the most noticeable overall phenomenon was a kind of flaking process, of dead ends, of self-cancelling propositions, of one concept confounded by another. The results do not add up to a neat and logical and defensible summary conclusion. But a powerful impression remains, best expressed in a letter written by Professor Kalven: "Our over-all impression . . . is that the jury is a pretty stubborn, healthy institution not likely to be overwhelmed either by a remark of counsel or a remark in the press."[2] To which is added the thought: Could it be that the American jury confounds all the subtle nuances of the behavioral sciences and simply does its duty? If this thought were cast into a series of hypotheses and subsequently confirmed by behavioral science, the jury trial would become even more firmly embedded in the ethos of American justice. While this is not very likely, a massive attack by the behavioral sciences on the *specific targets* involved could go far toward answering the problem posed at the outset of this review: Do some kinds of pretrial publicity under some kinds of conditions have some kinds of influence upon some kinds of jurors with a scientifically measurable effect upon jury verdicts? The free press/fair trial controversy—which is in effect a battle between two good guys, a battle that diminishes both—would then become amenable to a rational solution within a framework of specific detail.

REFERENCES CITED

BOOKS

ADORNO, T. W., *et al., The Authoritarian Personality* (New York: Harper & Brothers, 1950).

ALLPORT, GORDON W., *The Nature of Prejudice* (Garden City: Doubleday, 1958).

[2] Quoted in Donald M. Gillmor, "Free Press and Fair Trial. . ." *North Dakota Law Review*, 41:156–76 (1965).

BARTLETT, FREDERIC C., *Remembering* (Cambridge: Cambridge University Press, 1932).

BERELSON, BERNARD, and GARY A. STEINER, *Human Behavior* (New York: Harcourt, Brace & World, 1964).

BERELSON, BERNARD, PAUL F. LAZARSFELD and WILLIAM N. MCPHEE, *Voting* (Chicago: University of Chicago Press, 1954).

BURDICK, EUGENE and A. J. BRODBECK, eds., *American Voting Behavior* (Glencoe, Illinois: Free Press, 1959).

BUSH, CHILTON R., *Newswriting and Reporting Public Affairs* (Philadelphia: Chilton Books, 1965).

CANTRIL, HADLEY, ed., *Gauging Public Opinion* (Princeton: Princeton University Press, 1944).

INSKO, CHESTER A., *Theories of Attitude Change* (New York: Appleton-Century-Crofts, 1967).

JONES, EDWARD E., and HAROLD B. GERARD, *Foundations of Social Psychology* (New York: John Wiley, 1967).

KALVEN, HARRY, JR., and HANS ZEISEL, *The American Jury* (Boston: Little, Brown, 1966).

KATZ, ELIHU and PAUL F. LAZARSFELD, *Personal Influence* (Glencoe, Illinois: Free Press, 1955).

KLAPPER, JOSEPH T., *The Effects of Mass Communications* (New York: Free Press, 1960).

LAZARSFELD, PAUL, BERNARD BERELSON and HAZEL GAUDET, *The People's Choice* (New York: Columbia University Press, 1948).

LIPPMANN, WALTER, *Public Opinion* (New York: Macmillan, 1922).

MURPHY, GARDNER, LOIS BARCLAY MURPHY and THEODORE M. NEWCOMB, *Experimental Social Psychology* (New York: Harper, 1937).

ROKEACH, MILTON, *The Open and Closed Mind* (New York: Basic Books, 1960).

TAGIURI, RENATO, and LUIGI PETRULLO, eds., *Person Perception and Interpersonal Behavior* (Stanford: Stanford University Press, 1958).

ARTICLES

ANNIS, ALBERT D., and NORMAN C. MEIER, "The Induction of Opinion Through Suggestion by Means of Planted Content," *The Journal of Social Psychology,* 5:65–79 (1934).

ASCH, SOLOMON E., "Forming Impressions of Personality," *The Journal of Abnormal Psychology,* 41:258–90 (1946).

ASCH, SOLOMON E., "Opinions and Social Pressure," *Scientific American,* 193:31–38 (1955).

BROEDER, DALE W., "Voir Dire Examinations: An Empirical Study," *Southern California Law Review,* 38:503–28 (1965).

Dow, Thomas E., Jr., "The Role of Identification in Conditioning Public Attitude Toward the Offender," *The Journal of Criminal Law, Criminology and Police Service,* 58:75–79.

Freedman, Jonathan L., and David O. Sears, "Warning, Distraction and Resistance to Influence," *Journal of Personality and Social Psychology,* 1:262–66 (1965).

Gillmor, Donald M., "Free Press and Fair Trial: A Continuing Dialogue [—] Trial by Newspaper and the Social Sciences," *North Dakota Law Review,* 41:156–76 (1965).

Goggin, Terrence P., and George M. Hanover, "Fair Trial v. Free Press: The Psychological Effect of Pre-Trial Publicity on the Juror's Ability to be Impartial: A Plea for Reform," *Southern California Law Review,* 38:672–88 (1965).

Hovland, Carl I., and Walter Weiss, "The Influence of Source Credibility on Communication Effectiveness," *Public Opinion Quarterly,* 15: 635–50 (1951).

Jaffee, Carolyn, "The Press and the Oppressed—A Study of Prejudical News Reporting in Criminal Cases," *The Journal of Criminal Law, Criminology and Police Service,* 56:1–17 (1965).

Kelley, Harold H., "The Warm-Cold Variable in First Impressions of Persons," *Journal of Personality,* 18:431–39 (1950).

Kelman, Herbert C., and Carl I. Hovland, " 'Reinstatement' of the Communicator in Delayed Measurement of Opinion Change," *Journal of Abnormal and Social Psychology,* 48:327–35 (1953).

Klapper, Joseph T. and Charles Y. Glock, "Trial by Newspaper," *Scientific American,* 180:16–21 (1949).

Kline, F. Gerald, and Paul H. Jess, "The Effect of Prejudical Publicity on Mock Juries at the University of Minnesota," a paper presented before Association for Education in Journalism, Syracuse, N.Y., August, 1965.

Kline, F. Gerald, and Paul H. Jess, "Prejudicial Publicity: Its Effect on Law School Mock Juries," *Journalism Quarterly,* 43:113–16 (1966).

McGuire, William J., "Inducing Resistance to Persuasion," in Leonard Berkowitz, ed., *Advances in Experimental Social Psychology* (New York: Academic Press, 1964).

Menzel, Herbert, and Elihu Katz, "Social Relations and Innovation in the Medical Profession," *Public Opinion Quarterly,* 19:337–52 (1955).

Millspaugh, Martin, "Trial by Mass Media?" *Public Opinion Quarterly,* 13:328–29 (1949).

Norris, Eleanor L., "Attitude Change as a Function of Open or Closed Mindedness," *Journalism Quarterly,* 42:571–75 (1965).

ROKEACH, MILTON, "Attitude Change and Behavioral Change," *Public Opinion Quarterly,* 30:529–50 (1966–67).

ROSNOW, R. L., "Whatever Happened to the Law of Primacy," *Journal of Communications,* 16:10–31. (1966).

SCHUR, EDWIN M., "Scientific Method and the Criminal Trial Decision," *Social Research,* 25:173–90 (1958).

SEARS, DAVID O., and JONATHAN F. FREEDMAN, "Selective Exposure to Information: A Critical Review," *Public Opinion Quarterly,* 31:194–213 (1967).

SEARS, DAVID O., JONATHAN L. FREEDMAN and EDWARD F. O'CONNOR, JR., "The Effects of Anticipated Debate and Commitment on the Polarization of Audience Opinion," *Public Opinion Quarterly,* 28:615–27 (1964).

SIMON, RITA JAMES, "Murder, Juries and the Press," *Trans-Action,* May–June, 1967.

STRODTBECK, FRED L., RITA M. JAMES and CHARLES HAWKINS, "Social Status in Jury Deliberations," *American Sociological Review,* 22:713–19 (1957).

TANS, MARY DEE, and STEVEN H. CHAFFEE, "Pretrial Publicity and Juror Prejudice," *Journalism Quarterly,* 43:647–54 (1966).

WILCOX, WALTER, and MAXWELL MCCOMBS, "Crime Story Elements and Fair Trial/Free Press," unpublished manuscript, UCLA, Los Angeles (1967).

WILCOX, WALTER, "Right of Reply in the United States," *Gazette,* 34:1–6 (1968).

CASES

Irvin v. *Dowd:* 81 S.Ct. 1639 (1961).
Rideaux v. *Louisiana:* 83 S.Ct. 294 (1963), 83 S.Ct. 1417 (1963).
Sheppard v. *Maxwell:* 86 S.Ct. 1507 (1966).
Stroble v. *California:* 343 U.S. 181 (1952).
United States v. *Alger Hiss,* In the United States Court of Appeals for the Second Circuit (on Appeal from the District Court of the United States for the Southern District of New York); Transcript of Record, Volume I, Notice of Motion for Change of Venue.

... IV ...

Access by Newsmen to Judicial Proceedings

FRED S. SIEBERT

THE question of whether newsmen representing the media of mass communication can attend and report various types of judicial proceedings continues to be debated in both judicial and journalistic circles. In recent years the problem has become even more acute with demands from the electronic media for permission to report judicial proceedings with the tools of their trade—television cameras and recording equipment.

Pencil reporters have been permitted to attend most types of judicial proceedings since the end of the 18th century. However, the "right" of reporters to be present at these proceedings has never been firmly established. The constitutional "right to a public trial" has been interpreted as a right of the defendant on trial and not necessarily a right of the press.

An attempt was made in the national survey of trial judges sponsored by the American Newspapers Association Foundation to determine what the actual practice is in trial courts and to elicit the judges' opinions on these practices. The sample of 483 trial judges was asked a number of questions concerning the practice in their jurisdictions.

The first question asked of the judges was whether news photographers were permitted access to the courtroom for the purpose of taking pictures during criminal proceedings. The answers are given in Table 1.

It would appear that the practice of prohibiting taking still pictures in the courtroom is practically universal.

A more controversial issue is whether photographers should be

Table 1

	Number of judges	Percent
Photographers permitted	25	5.2
Photographers not permitted	451	93.3
No answer	7	1.4

permitted to take pictures within the courtroom building (corridors, etc.) or on the courthouse grounds.

The answers of trial judges to the question whether photographers are permitted to take pictures within the courthouse building or on the courthouse grounds are found in Table 2.

Table 2

	Number of judges	Percent
Photographs permitted in courthouse and grounds	335	69.3
Photographs permitted on grounds but not in building	17	3.5
No photographs either in buildings or grounds	63	13.0
Not applicable or no answer	67	14.0

The sample of judges was then asked whether in their opinion news photographers *should* be permitted to take pictures in the courtroom during criminal proceedings. The answers are found in Table 3.

Table 3

	Number of judges	Percent
Photographs should not be permitted in courtroom	427	88.4
Photographs should be permitted	47	9.7
No answer	9	1.0

To the question, *should* news photographers be permitted to take pictures within the court building (but not in the courtroom) or on the courthouse grounds, the judges' answers are contained in Table 4.

As a result of the almost universal ban on courtroom pictures, a number of newspapers as well as radio and television stations have

Table 4

	Number of judges	Percent
Pictures should be permitted in court building or on ground	280	59.9
No pictures in building or on grounds	103	21.2
No answer	100	20.6

assigned artists to make sketches in the courtroom during well-publicized criminal trials.

The trial judges were asked whether such sketching was permitted in their courtrooms during criminal trials. The answers are presented in Table 5.

Table 5

	Number of judges	Percent
Sketching permitted	259	53.6
Sketching not permitted	190	39.3
No answer	34	7.0

The question whether television cameras should be permitted to cover criminal trial proceedings has been debated in both judicial and journalistic circles. The trial judges' answers as to whether television cameras were permitted in their courtrooms during criminal proceedings are found in Table 6.

Table 6

	Number of judges	Percent
Television cameras not permitted	467	96.6
Television cameras permitted	6	1.2
No answer	10	2.0

A few more judges would seem to permit news photographers to take pictures in the courtroom (5.1%) than would permit television cameras (1.2%).

When asked whether in their opinion television cameramen should be permitted to take pictures in the courtroom during criminal trials, only twenty-three judges (4.7%), gave an affirmative answer. Four hundred and forty-five judges (92%) would ban television cameras in the courtroom. Fifteen judges did not answer.

Again the judges were asked whether they permit television cameras to take pictures within the courthouse building or on the courthouse grounds. The answers are found in Table 7.

Table 7

	Number of judges	Percent
TV pictures permitted in courthouse and on grounds	362	74.9
TV pictures permitted on grounds but not in buildings	17	3.5
No TV pictures either in building or on grounds	86	17.7
Not applicable or no answer	18	3.6

The differences between the figures in the above Table 7 and Table 2 (access by news photographers) apparently is accounted for by the fact that a smaller number of judges appears in the "no answer" column in Table 7 than in Table 2.

In answer to the question whether TV cameramen *should* be permitted to take pictures within the courthouse or on the courthouse grounds or both, the judges answered as follows in Table 8.

Table 8

	Number of judges	Percent
TV pictures should be permitted in court building and on grounds	331	68.5
TV pictures should not be permitted in court building or on grounds	117	24.2
TV pictures should be permitted on grounds but not in building	14	2.8
No answer	18	3.6

A considerably larger number of judges (100 as compared with 18) were reluctant to express themselves on the question of access by still photographers to the courthouse and court grounds (see Table 4) than were willing to give an opinion on whether TV cameramen should have access to these same sites.

A more specific problem which continues to arise across the country is whether reporters (pencil) are permitted to attend and report preliminary hearings in criminal cases. When queried on this question, the sample of trial judges hearing felony cases reported as follows in Table 9.

Table 9

	Number of judges	Percent
Reporters permitted to report preliminary hearings	375	77.6
Reporters not permitted to report preliminary hearings	18	3.7
Not applicable; no preliminary hearings	89	18.4
No answer	1	.2

When asked whether reporters *should* be permitted to report preliminary hearings in criminal cases, the sample of judges answered is shown in Table 10.

Table 10

	Number of judges	Percent
Reporters should be permitted to report preliminary hearings	391	80.9
On certain occasions	5	1.0
Reporters should not be permitted to report preliminary hearings	64	13.2
No answer	23	4.7

SUMMARY

The practice of denying permission to all types of photographers (still and TV) to take pictures in the courtroom during the progress of a criminal trial is practically universal. Only 9.7 percent of the trial judges felt that photographers should be permitted in the courtroom.

Most judges queried would permit pictures to be taken on the courthouse grounds and within the courthouse building.

Sketching in the courtroom during the trial is permitted by more than one-half of the judges.

Only 18 of the 483 judges said that reporters were not permitted to attend and report preliminary hearing in criminal cases while 64 judges contended that reporters should not be present at arraignments and preliminary hearings.

... V ...

What We Have Learned

CHILTON R. BUSH

THE Detroit study was done to obtain some exact evidence of the magnitude of the problem in terms of felony crimes, jury trials of the crimes, and newspaper reports of the crimes. The city of Detroit was selected because of its convenience for Mr. Hough and because of the efficiency of the data analysis of the municipal court system. There is good reason for believing that the Detroit findings with respect to both the crime data and the frequency of news reports of crimes are so typical that an analysis of data in other cities would add little to our knowledge.

Mr. Hough found that of the 9,140 felony cases disposed of by the Recorder's Court in the calendar year of 1967, only 3.4 percent had gone to jury trial and only 2.4 percent resulted in a verdict of guilty. He also found that of the felony cases for which warrants had been issued in a six-month period, only 7 percent had been reported in the Detroit *Free Press*, and that nearly one-half of all crimes reported in that paper were from outside the state of Michigan.[1]

Of course, the objection may be made that the magnitude of the problem should be measured not by mere numbers but by the sensational cases and by the content of the news stories reporting them.[2] In very recent years, however, it would be difficult to cite

---

1. Clifton Daniel has mentioned a count made in New York City in 1965 which found that of 11,724 felonies committed in January, only 41 were reported in the New York *Daily News*. —American Society of Newspaper Editors, *Problems of Journalism, 1965*, p. 111.

2. See Telford Taylor, *Two Studies in Constitutional Interpretation:* Columbus, Ohio, 1969, pp. 138-40. This lecture includes an excellent presentation of historical background on the problem dating from 1846.

such cases. If we disregard the recent assassinations of important public persons, which the public must know about, there have been few such cases. In connection with the sensational Candace Mossler trial in Miami in 1966, for example, the Associated Press examined 112 issues of newspapers from different parts of the country for two days. Of these, 12 carried the story on the first page, 35 did not use the story at all, and 65 published the story on inside pages allocating from two paragraphs to one column.[3]

There are two reasons for this low emphasis of a sensational crime: (1) in this serious era, such news is competing with news of greater social importance, and (2) few newspapers are competing with each other for street sales. It would seem that the problem of pretrial publicity in the United States is of much less magnitude than it was some years ago. This contrasts with the situation in England, where the popular national newspapers have a larger audience for sensational news because of the statutory school-leaving age of 15 years and the robust competition among such newspapers.

JUDGES' OPINIONS

One reason for making the study of judges' opinions was the inadequacy of some of the research data developed by the American Bar Association Advisory Committee on Fair Trial and Free Press.[4] In that study, questionnaires were mailed to 200 judges; only 68 (34 percent), for example, responded to the question about the efficacy of continuance. Nothing is known from that data about the opinions of the 132 judges who did not respond. In the present study, which was done by personal interview, every judge had an equal chance of being selected in the sample and nearly all who had heard felony cases stated an opinion.

Unanimity is almost never a characteristic of opinion and attitude studies: the data nearly always form a continuum. This is true of the present study and was to be expected.

Interpretation in many studies is assisted by certain explanatory data that emerge from voluntary comments, responses to certain "why" questions, and from cross-tabulation of certain responses.

3. *AP Log*, February 2-8, 1966 and March 23-29, 1966. See also George Beebe, "Is the Big Murder Trial Passé?", *Bulletin of the American Society of Newspaper Editors*, April 1, 1966, and *AP Log*, July 27-August 2, 1970, about the sensational Manson trial in Los Angeles.

4. Standards Relating to Fair Trial and Free Press; A.B.A. Project on Minimum Standards for Criminal Justice (1964).

In this study, however, there is little explanatory data and the reader is forced to speculation.

How, for example, should one interpret Table 6 (Frequency of Accepting Jurors Who Say They Have Learned About the Case From Published Reports)? Forty percent of the judges said they always or most of the time accept jurors who admit they have learned about the case from published reports, and 20.7 percent said they practically never do so. Does this mean that 40 percent feel confident that jurors will put aside the knowledge they brought to the court and consider only the admissible evidence, and that one-fifth of the judges lack that confidence?

Or as to the judges' opinions about the efficacy of *voir dire*, do we find any support for the proposition that a good many judges believe that jurors in their deliberations ignore their previous knowledge? Table 11 shows that 44.3 percent believe that *voir dire* is highly effective and only 4.5 percent believe it is ineffective.

The judges were asked how frequently in widely reported cases where the jury has not been sequestered they had admonished jurors not to read or listen to reports about the trial (Question 4-D). Exactly 81.7 percent said they "always or nearly always" admonished the jurors. Yet 27.9 percent of those who gave that response said they had reason to believe that, on some occasions, the admonition had not been complied with (Question 4-E: "In a situation of this type have you *ever* had reason to believe that your admonition was not complied with?"). Do the judges who gave that answer regard admonition as a perfunctory procedure, or did they have in mind only one of a very few instances of noncompliances? Table 13 shows that only 15.3 percent thought that admonition was ineffective.

Or what can we say about the judges' evaluation of sequestration? More than 60 percent of the judges who had used the procedure think it is highly effective and only 13.1 percent think it is ineffective (Table 12). Yet 43.8 percent say they "practically never" sequester (Table 9). Does this mean that the judges who seldom use this procedure believe that jurors are not influenced by what they read or hear during a trial or are reluctant to inconvenience jurors?

From the data about other safeguards, we learn that about three-fourths of the judges think they are either highly or moderately effective. Almost half of the judges, however, think that habeas corpus after conviction is an ineffective safeguard.

How may we interpret the judges' responses to this question: "Would you agree or disagree with this statement (made recently by a judge): 'The ultimate blame for failure of a fair trial that goes uncorrected must . . . rest upon the judiciary. Show me an unfair trial that goes uncorrected and I will show you a judge who has failed in his duty' "?

This is an admission that is not easy for a judge to make. Yet 58.1 percent agreed and 38.7 percent disagreed; 15 judges (3.2 percent) did not answer. We do not know the context in which the judges considered the question. It was asked near the end of the interview and we might suppose that most of the judges, in considering their response, reviewed their answers to the previous questions so that their response to this question was a summary conclusion for which they had been oriented by all of the previous questions. If that is true, then we might be safe in inferring that a majority of the judges had a good deal of confidence in the jury system as they have observed it from their own experience.

A series of questions was asked as to whether it was "appropriate or inappropriate" for law enforcement authorities to release to the press the content of a confession, the results of tests, etc., and for the news media to publish the prior criminal record of a defendant. The "generally inappropriate" response to the first two questions approached unanimity and for publication of the criminal record was 86.3 percent. The latter percentage, however, was reduced to 61.2 percent when the question was formulated in a concrete, rather than a general, sense (Question 19: "The criminal record of the alleged assassin of Martin Luther King has been widely publicized. In this particular case, would you say that such publicity is appropriate or inappropriate?"); also the percentage of "appropriate" responses increased from 6.6 percent to 21.6 percent.

If the judges who gave both kinds of responses to the concrete question had been asked why they had responded in the way they did, we might have obtained an explanation of their reasoning. What, for example, was appropriate for release to the press about Dr. King's alleged assassin? Attorney-General Ramsey Clark announced in June, 1968, James Earl Ray's arrest at a London airport. Immediately it became known that Ray had escaped from a Missouri prison and had thirteen years remaining of his term of confinement. The F.B.I., Scotland Yard, Canadian police, and Ray's brother answered a good many questions put to them by newsmen. These were questions that trained newsmen knew had arisen in the minds of readers, and correct answers were needed to reduce the ambiguity of the situation. Rumor thrives in the absence of standards of evidence because the human mind finds it impossible to accept ambiguity. The mind must believe something; as psychologists say, the mind "makes an effort after meaning." Even the findings of the authoritative Warren Commission were not accepted by some people, and some skepticism has persisted in the Ray case because Ray pleaded guilty before much evidence had been presented at his trial. The best time to stifle rumor in situations of this kind is at the time of arrest, not several months later.[5] We can only speculate that some judges who were interviewed either were not aware of this necessity or did not believe there was the necessity.

It is a commonplace in opinion and attitude research that some respondents give conflicting answers to general and to concrete questions.[6] There is an apparent inconsistency in the data in Tables 7 and 24. In the latter table, 96.4 percent of the judges said it is "generally inappropriate" for law enforcement officers to release the content of a confession in advance of a trial (Question 13). Yet in Table 7, 36 percent had previously said they practically never sustain a challenge for cause when a venireman admits he has read that the defendant had confessed to the crime (Question 4-D). Since jurors usually decide whether or not a confession was made voluntarily and, if the confession is admitted as evidence, whether or not it is true, a good many judges, according to the data, would seem to think that the juror disregards what he has read. It would seem that the judges' answers in a concrete situation are a more reliable measure of their opinion than their responses to a highly general question. However, 39.4 percent said they practically always sustain the challenge and 13.8 percent said they do most of the time.

Press-Bar Agreements

At the time that judges were interviewed (June, 1968) only 14.9 percent reported that a press-bar agreement was in effect in their "community." By early 1970, however, such agreements were in effect in 22 states and were being negotiated in 10 other states. In the "communities" in which such an agreement was in effect when the judges were interviewed 87.5 percent said that performance under the agreements was "good." Of all the judges who were interviewed, more than 50 percent approved such agreements and 19.4 percent did not feel that an agreement was the answer.

---

5. Justice Black said in the majority opinion in the Bridges and Times-Mirror cases with reference to comment but true *a fortiori* as to facts: "Discussion during pendency of a case comes at precisely the time when it might do the most good. . . . The judgments below, therefore, produce their restrictive results at the precise time when public interest in the matters discussed would naturally be at its height." —314 U. S. 252, 1941.

6. For example: general: "Do you (a Caucasian) think that Negroes and whites should be treated equally?" "Yes." And concrete: "Would you object or not object to living next door to a Negro?" "I would object."

In several communities an agreement will be of great value to newspapers in educating certain public officials as to workable policies. One example is the rural sheriff who is an influential member of a courthouse political organization and who sometimes uses inflexible rules to make himself a little dictator.

The free press-fair trial controversy seems to have demonstrated that there was a certain amount of ignorance on the part of the press, bar, and bench of each others' duties and procedures and of the consequences of publishing or not publishing certain facts. This lack of understanding can be reduced by statewide agreements because most of the principles and guidelines explicitly or implicitly provide for a program of education for all parties and, in several instances, for the bench-bar-press committee to serve as an advisory clearinghouse and evaluation review board with respect to specific trials, either terminated or scheduled.

Possibly the oldest such agreement was adopted in 1927 by the Burlington, Vermont, newspapers and the judge of the City Court, the initiative having been taken by the late Judge Clarence P. Cowles. One of the parties to the agreement, Robert Beaupre, a reporter for the *Free Press* at the time, has recently said of Judge Cowles:

"No municipal judges then wore judicial robes. But Judge Cowles did. He wanted to lend dignity to the court. Always he emphasized this dignity and sought to have it maintained in the press.

"During those days of unpopular prohibition, the judge heard many bootlegging cases and fantastic disclosures in intoxication cases. Remarks and scenes before the bench were sometimes disparaging. Judge Cowles wanted these reported temperately lest the public image of the court suffer. But this called only for the restraint of seasoned reporting in a good conservative daily; never for suppression; never for omission of details that might tend to deter crime.

"He felt strongly that the people had the right to know, that the court always should be open for the good of the defendant and public."

The 1927 agreement which Judge Cowles initiated is reproduced in the Appendix.

SEARCH OF THE LITERATURE

In his search of the literature, Dr. Wilcox found four studies in which subjects had been exposed to simulated pretrial publicity (one was a civil case) and evaluated them. He found they "fall short of the mark" because they were done in an artificial setting or in a simulated situation or because the experimental design did not include all of the mediating variables present in an actual trial.

Dr. Wilcox also made an exhaustive search of the experimental literature of the behavioral sciences looking for theories and concepts which could have application in a jury trial situation. He concluded that, in applying them, the research techniques were not, collectively, sensitive enough to justify linkage to a real situation.

His explanation for the low power of the experimental evidence is that few of the experiments had been oriented to the uniqueness of the jury system whereas in the fields of learning, marketing, etc. they had been "on point." He concluded, however, that a massive attack by the behavioral sciences on specific targets could go far toward answering the question.

Outside of the experimental literature of the behavioral sciences, Dr. Wilcox found some evidence that knowledge by jurors of the defendant's criminal record could have some potency. The evidence— from *The Chicago Jury Project*—was the inference by several judges that the jury would not have acquitted if it had known of the defendant's prior criminal record, which the judges knew about; and statistical data that the defendant with a criminal record who does not testify is less likely to be acquitted than the defendant without a record who does testify.

One of the areas for further research suggested by Dr. Wilcox is the effect of the admonition to jurors not to discuss what they have heard or read prior to the trial. It would seem that a test of this aspect of the problem, considered by itself without reference to other variables, could develop a reliable and valid finding as to jury behavior, for Dr. Siebert's survey of judges disclosed the need for more objective evidence.

A second area for research, discussed by Dr. Wilcox only in terms of theory, are diffusion and retention. It would seem feasible, in connection with one or more dramatic crimes reported by the press, to test immediately after the report the amount and the form of detail learned by potential jurors (diffusion) and, at a later stage, to ascertain the amount and form of the detail that was reinstated in the memory of those who had heard or read about the case (retention).

From these studies we have learned a great deal about the value to all concerned in communications between the press on the one hand and the bench and bar on the other. Where such communications have taken place there has been mutual understanding and a reduction in the controversy. All of this is in the public interest.

Appendices

Some Press-Bench-Bar Agreements

The City Court and The Press

Burlington, Vermont, Adopted in 1927

I. THE PRESS AND THE CITY COURT

The Observance of Law

The City Court in a special way represents law and order in the community. The Press can render large service in helping maintain general observance of law by wielding the power of its influence in creating and maintaining due respect for the City Court.

"The ultimate object of the proper administration of criminal justice is to sustain and increase the general respect for law." —ARTHUR TRAIN.

Respect for Courts

Sensational, flippant or vulgar publicity weakens courts of justice in their influence and in their hold upon the respect of the citizens, good and bad.

The dignity of its function merits due respect, but the judge must maintain the dignity of the court and make it worthy of respect.

"Unbecoming situations may usually be ignored or indulged. All courts, weak or normal, are entitled to be dealt with so far as they themselves make it possible, as the dignified and solemn functionaries of the government." —ANDREW R. SHERIFF.

Informative Reporting

The report should be informative to the thoughtful, giving as full information as desired respecting the work and acts of the court, with reasons given therefor.

"Assuredly, anything which tends to direct the interest of the layman to the actual principles of the law and the mode of administering justice in the courts is greatly to be desired. The layman has no more essential interest than the function of the courts." —EDITOR OF *American Bar Association Journal.*

It supports the court to give reasons for its acts, and so make the court seem reasonable and just.

Accuracy is of course a first requisite.

"That the public should see and feel that justice is done is scarcely less important than the actual doing of justice." —DEAN POUND

The Court, Not the Judge

Emphasis should be placed upon the court as a whole, as an impersonal institution of government. The personality of the judge should be kept in the background.

This court is the "City Court," and the judge is the "City Judge."

Children and the Family

Publicity concerning children and intimate family relations, especially abnormal family conditions, should generally be avoided.

Making either heroes or villians out of youthful offenders is likely to be harmful.

In England the law prohibits publication of testimony in all divorce cases. In Vermont this is discretionary with the court (G. L. 3574). The spirit of this rule applies to the criminal court.

Sordid Details

Make crime repulsive. Show the misery that goes with wrongdoing. But sordid and degrading details will of course be omitted.

Publicity Before Trial

Caution will be exercised in reporting lengthy stories before court hearing. This may wrongfully affect the court trial, and duplicating the story of a crime may unduly emphasize it in the community.

Prosecuting officers and attorneys should not try their cases in the newspapers before court.

Publicity Helps Check Crime

When crime is prevalent and not duly repressed, vigorous publicity supports the law enforcement officers, warns would-be offenders and greatly helps check the crime.

To repress crime bring it out into the light of day. Like microbes, crime cannot live in the sunlight.

The greater publicity should be given to those crimes which are most harmful to the community, and in which aid is most needed in their repression. The actual interest of the public is not always the best guide.

The Great Ends

The great ends to be kept steadily in view in all press reporting of the criminal court are the prevention and repression of crime, the maintenance of law and order, and the establishment of justice. The Press is the strong ally of the criminal court in the achievement of these, the primary and chief ends of government.

The making of a good story is often a commendable, but not the highest aim in criminal court reporting.

II. THE CITY COURT AND THE PRESS

The Open Court

It is a fundamental principle of Anglo-Saxon jurisprudence that courts must be kept open to public view. This is for the good of the courts and in the interest of the administration of justice and good government, as well as to give the accused his constitutional right to a public hearing. This rule has special force in the criminal branch of the court. Criminal cases are "state" cases, i.e. *public* cases. In their very nature, crimes are those acts which are specially harmful to the public. The public has the deepest interest in criminal cases.

The Press in a very special way represents the public in the court room. It is the eyes and ears of the public.

The principle of the open court is of great practical importance. It should be followed in spirit and in truth. To that end the Press should be given proper facilities for observing court proceedings. The court should be held at regular stated times so that representatives of the Press may have fair opportunity to attend. Conferences in the Judge's room and whispering at the bench tend to set up a secret court and with few exceptions should be avoided. The Press and the public are entitled to know all that is done in a court, especially in a criminal court.

Minors shall, and all persons may be excluded when a cause of scandalous or obscene nature is on trial (G. L. 1485).

The clerk, judge, attorneys and all officers of the court will assist the representatives of the Press in securing full and accurate information respecting all court proceedings.

"In this country it is a first principle that the people have the right to know what is done in their courts." —*In re Shortridge,* 99 Cal. 529, 21 L. R. A. 755.

The Freedom of the Press

"That the people have a right to freedom of speech, and of writing and publishing their sentiments, concerning the transactions of government, and therefore the freedom of the press ought not to be restrained."—Art. 13, Constitution of Vermont.

The responsibility for publishing or not publishing any court proceedings is upon the Press. The court records and proceedings are public. No officer of the court will try to conceal any court record or action from the Press, or try to have it suppressed by the Press.

Fair, respectful criticism of a court is permissible, but should be cautiously done for fear of weakening the court. The strongest possible criminal courts are none too strong to cope adequately with the forces of evil.

Defaming or scandalizing a court or judge respecting any court action, or unjustly bringing the court or its judge into contempt and weakening its authority, is a contempt of court.—*State v. Hildreth,* 82 Vt. 382; G. L. 7026.

"It is of first importance to the improvement of our legal system, therefore, that our legal institutions and their functioning should be justly, fairly and intelligently interpreted to the people." —Harland F. Stone, Justice of United States Supreme Court.

Recommended Guidelines of
The Fair Trial-Free Press Council of Minnesota
Relating to Adult Criminal Proceedings

I

The following information generally *should* be made public at or immediately following the time of arrest:

(A) The Accused's name, age, residence, employment, marital status and similar background information.

(B The substance or text of the charge, such as is or would be contained in a complaint, indictment, or information.

(C) The identity of the investigating and arresting agency and the length of the investigation.

(D) The circumstances immediately surrounding an arrest, including the time and place of arrest, resistance, pursuit, possession and use of weapons, and a description of items seized at the time of arrest.

II

The following information generally *should not* be made public at or immediately after the time of arrest.

(A) Statements as to the character or reputation of an accused person.

(B) Existence of contents of any confession, admission, or statement given by the accused, or his refusal to make a statement.

(C) Performance or results of tests, or the refusal of an accused to take such a test.

(D) Expected content of testimony, or credibility of prospective witnesses.

(E) Possibility of a plea of guilty to the offense charged or to a lesser offense, or other disposition.

(F) Other statements relating to the merits, evidence, argument, opinions, or theories of the case.

Oregon State Bar-Press-Broadcasters
Joint Statement of Principles

Oregon's Bill of Rights provides both for fair trials and for freedom of the press. These rights are basic and unqualified. They are not ends in themselves but are necessary guarantors of freedom for the individual and the public's rights to be informed. The necessity of preserving both the right to fair trial and the freedom to disseminate the news is of concern to responsible members of the legal and journalistic professions and is of equal concern to the public. At times these two rights appear to be in conflict with each other.

In an effort to mitigate this conflict, the Oregon State Bar, the Oregon Newspaper Publishers Association and the Oregon Association of Broadcasters have adopted the following statement of principles to keep the public fully informed without violating the rights of any individual.

1. The news media have the right and the responsibility to print and to broadcast the truth.

2. However, the demands of accuracy and objectivity in news reporting should be balanced with the demands of fair play. The public has a right to be informed. The accused has the right to be judged in an atmosphere free from undue prejudice.

3. Good taste should prevail in the selection, printing and broadcasting of the news. Morbid or sensational details of criminal behavior should not be exploited.

4. The right to decision about the news rests with the editor or news director. In the exercise of judgment he should consider that:

    (a) an accused person is presumed innocent until proved guilty.

    (b) readers and listeners are potential jurors;

    (c) no person's reputation should be injured needlessly.

5. The public is entitled to know how justice is being administered. However, it is unprofessional for any lawyer to exploit any medium of public information to enhance his side of a pending case. It follows that the public prosecutor should avoid taking unfair advantage of his position as an important source of news; this shall not be construed to limit his obligation to make available information to which the public is entitled.

In recognition of these principles, the undersigned hereby testify to their continuing desire to achieve the best possible accommodation of the rights of the individual and the rights of the public when these two fundamental precepts appear to be in conflict in the administration of justice.

GUIDELINES FOR DISCLOSURE AND REPORTING OF INFORMATION ON CRIMINAL PROCEEDINGS

It is generally appropriate to disclose or report the following:

1. The arrested person's name, age, residence, employment, marital status and similar biographical information.
2. The charge.
3. The amount of bail.
4. The identity of and biographical information concerning both complaining party and victim.
5. The identity of the investigating and arresting agency and the length of the investigation.
6. The circumstances of arrest, including time, place, resistance, pursuit and weapons used.

It is inappropriate to disclose for publication or to report prior to the trial the following:

1. The contents of any admission or confession, or the fact that an admission or confession has been made.
2. Opinions about an arrested person's character, guilt or innocence.
3. Opinions concerning evidence or argument in the case.
4. Statements concerning anticipated testimony or the truthfulness of prospective witnesses.
5. The results of fingerprints, polygraph examinations, ballistic tests or laboratory tests.
6. Precise descriptions of items seized or discovered during investigation.
7. Prior criminal charges and convictions.

PHOTOGRAPHY

1. Photographs of a suspect may be released by law enforcement personnel provided a valid law enforcement function is served. It is proper to disclose such information as may be necessary to enlist public assistance in apprehending fugitives from justice. Such disclosure may include photographs as well as records of prior arrests and convictions.
2. Law enforcement and court personnel should not prevent the photographing of defendants when they are in public places outside the courtroom. However, they should not pose the defendant.

Statement of Principles of the
Bench-Bar-Press of the State of Washington

PREAMBLE

The Bench, Bar and Press (comprising all media of mass communications) of Washington:

(a) Recognize that freedom of news media is one of the fundamental liberties guaranteed by the First Amendment of the Constitution of the United States and that this basic freedom must be zealously preserved and responsibly exercised.

(b) Are obliged to preserve the principle of the presumption of innocence for those accused of a crime until there has been a finding of guilt in an appropriate court of justice.

(c) Believe members of an organized society have the right to acquire and impart information about their mutual interests. The right to disseminate information should be exercised with discretion when public disclosures might jeopardize the ends of justice.

(d) Have the responsibility to support the free flow of information, consistent with the principles of the Constitution and this Preamble.

To promote a better understanding between the Bench and Bar of Washington and the Washington News Media, particularly in their efforts to reconcile the constitutional guarantee of freedom of the press and the right to a fair, impartial trial, the following statement of principles, mutually drawn and submitted for voluntary compliance, is recommended to all members of these professions in Washington.

PRINCIPLES

1. The News Media have the right and responsibility to print the truth. A free and responsible news media enhances the administration of justice. Members of the Bench and Bar should, within their respective canons of Legal ethics, cooperate with the news media in the reporting of the administration of justice.

2. Parties to litigation have the right to have their causes tried fairly by an impartial tribunal. Defendants in criminal cases are guaranteed this right by the Constitutions of the United States and the various states.

3. No trial should be influenced by the pressure of publicity from news media nor from public clamor, and lawyers and journalists share the responsibility to prevent the creation of such pressures.

4. All news media should strive for objectivity and accuracy. The

public has a right to be informed. The accused has a right to be judged in an atmosphere free from undue prejudice.

5. The news media recognizes the responsibility of the judge to preserve order in the court and to seek the ends of justice by all those means available to him.

6. Decisions about handling the news rest with editors, but in the exercise of news judgments the editor should remember that:

(a) An accused person is presumed innocent until proven guilty.

(b) Readers and listeners and viewers are potential jurors.

(c) No person's reputation should be injured needlessly.

7. The public is entitled to know how justice is being administered. However, no lawyer should exploit any medium of public information to enhance his side of a pending case. It follows that the public prosecutor should avoid taking unfair advantage of his position as an important source of news; this shall not be construed to limit his obligation to make available information to which the public is entitled.

8. Proper journalistic and legal training should include instruction in the meaning of constitutional rights to a fair trial, freedom of press, and the role of both journalist and lawyer in guarding these rights.

ADOPTED March 26, 1966, in general session, by a joint committee representing the following groups:

Washington State Supreme Court	Allied Daily Newspapers of Washington
Superior Court Judges' Association	Washington Newspaper Publishers Assn.
Washington State Magistrates' Assn.	Washington State Assn. of Broadcasters
Washington State Bar Association	The Associated Press
Washington Assn. of Sheriffs & Chiefs of Police	United Press-International
Washington State Prosecuting Attorneys' Association	School of Communications University of Washington

GUIDELINES FOR THE REPORTING OF CRIMINAL PROCEEDINGS

The proper administration of justice is the responsibility of the judiciary, bar, the prosecution, law enforcement personnel, news media and the public. None should relinquish its share in that responsibility or attempt to override or regulate the judgment of the other. None should condone injustices on the ground that they are infrequent.

The greatest news interest is usually engendered during the pretrial stage of a criminal case. It is then that the maximum attention is received and the greatest impact is made upon the public mind. It is then that the greatest danger to a fair trial occurs. The bench, the bar and the news media must exercise good judgment to balance the possible release of prejudicial information with the real public interest. However, these considerations are not necessarily applicable once a jury has been empaneled in a case. It is inherent in the concept of freedom of the press that the news media be free to report what occurs in public proceedings, such as criminal trials. In the course of the trial it is the responsibility of the bench to take appropriate measures to insure that the deliberations of the jury are based upon what is presented to them in court.

These guidelines are proposed as a means of balancing the public's right to be informed with the accused's right to a fair trial before an impartial jury.

1. It is appropriate to make public the following information concerning the defendant:

(a) The defendant's name, age, residence, employment, marital status, and similar background information. There should be no restraint on biographical facts other than accuracy, good taste and judgement.

(b) The substance or text of the charge, such as complaint, indictment, information or, where appropriate, the identity of the complaining party.

(c) The identity of the investigating and arresting agency and the length of the investigation.

(d) The circumstances immediately surrounding an arrest, including the time and place of arrest, resistance, pursuit, possession and use of weapons, and a description of items seized at the time of arrest.

2. The release of certain types of information by law enforcement personnel, the bench and bar and the publication thereof by news media generally tends to create dangers of prejudice without serving a significant law enforcement or public interest function. Therefore, all concerned should be aware of the dangers of prejudice in making pretrial public disclosures of the following:

(a) Opinions about a defendant's character, his guilt or innocence.

(b) Admissions, confessions or the contents of a statement or alibis attributable to a defendant.

(c) References to the results of investigative procedures, such as fingerprints, polygraph examinations, ballistic tests, or laboratory tests.

(d) Statements concerning the credibility or anticipated testimony of prospective witnesses.

(e) Opinions concerning evidence or argument in the case,

whether or not it is anticipated that such evidence or argument will be used at trial.

Exceptions may be in order if information to the public is essential to the apprehension of a suspect, or where other public interests will be served.

3. Prior criminal charges and convictions are matters of public record and are available to the news media through police agencies or court clerks. Law enforcement agencies should make such information available to the news media after a legitimate inquiry. The public disclosure of this information by the news media may be highly prejudicial without any significant addition to the public's need to be informed. The publication of such information should be carefully reviewed.

4. Law enforcement and court personnel should not prevent the photographing of defendants when they are in public places outside the courtroom. They should not encourage pictures or televising nor should they pose the defendant.

5. Photographs of a suspect may be released by law enforcement personnel provided a valid law enforcement function is served thereby. It is proper to disclose such information as may be necessary to enlist public assistance in apprehending fugitives from justice. Such disclosure may include photographs as well as records of prior arrests and convictions.

6. The news media are free to report what occurs in the course of the judicial proceedings itself. The bench should utilize available measures, such as cautionary instructions, sequestration of the jury and the holding of hearings on evidence after the empaneling of the jury, to insure that the jury's deliberations are based upon evidence presented to them in court.

7. It is improper for members of the bench-bar-news media or law enforcement agencies to make available to the public any statement or information for the purpose of influencing the outcome of a criminal trial.

8. Sensationalism should be avoided by all persons and agencies connected with the trial or reporting of a criminal case.

GUIDELINES ON THE REPORTING OF
JUVENILE COURT PROCEEDINGS

1. News media and judges should work together with confidence in, and respect for, each other.

2. News media should be welcome to all sessions of the juvenile court. If the privilege is exercised and cases are reported, news media

should not disclose names or identifying data of the participants unless authorized by the court. News media attending sessions of the juvenile court should make every effort to remain in attendance during all sessions of cases they intend to report.

3. The names and identifying data pertaining to alleged juvenile offenders may be used by the news media in those cases that are remanded by the juvenile court for criminal prosecution under adult standards.

4. Responsibility for developing sound public interest in and understanding of the child, the community, and the court must be shared by the judge and the news media.

5. All official records should be open to the news media with the judges' consent, unless inspection is prohibited by statute.

6. Confidential reports, such as social and clinical studies, school or personal records, should not be open to inspection by the press, except at the express order of the court.

7. The judge, at his discretion, may release the name or other identifying information of a juvenile offender in his court.

8. The court should strictly adhere to the Canons of Professional Ethics, which generally condemn the release of information concerning pending or anticipated judicial proceedings.

9. If an alleged act of delinquency is publicized, news media should be informed of the disposition of the case to complete the original story.

10. In the handling of juvenile matters the basic principles of fairness and cooperation summarized in the preamble and principles of the Bench-Bar-Press Committee of Washington shall apply. The possibility that any juvenile matter may ultimately be handled as a criminal case should be borne in mind.

11. Nothing in the foregoing guidelines shall be construed to prevent news media from exercising their constitutional right to publish any news about juvenile offenders from the time of their apprehension through the disposition of their cases if such information can be obtained from sources other than the courts, should the latter not wish to release such information.

a. In such instances due consideration should be given to recommendations of the juvenile court and its officers.

b. In determining whether to disclose names or other identifying data pertaining to alleged juvenile offenders, due consideration should be given as to whether that information is of the type the public must have to be fully aware of its juvenile court and the delinquency situation.

GUIDELINES ON THE REPORTING OF
CIVIL PROCEEDINGS

1. *The Need for Broader Coverage*: Although far more numerous than the trials in criminal courts, civil trials receive only a fraction of the attention devoted to criminal proceedings. One reason may be the brevity of the civil case; another may be its apparent lack of human interest. Judges and lawyers should recognize a third reason: that newsmen do not understand some civil proceedings and pass them up for want of sufficient time to study or do leg work.

The courts and their officers should give special attention to the need of the reporter to have background information and an interpretation of evidence as it is presented. Only the news media can give the public an objective and adequate explanation of civil actions and the reasons for judgments, orders and verdicts entered in such matters.

2. *Interpreting Legal Terms*: Judges and lawyers traditionally have employed legal phrases with special meaning to the profession. Unless these terms are interpreted faithfully by newsmen, the public cannot be expected to understand their significance. It is the duty of judicial officers and their staffs to assist representatives of the news media to report accurately in lay language. Written judicial decisions should be so drafted that selected portions briefly summarizing the court's ruling may be quoted by the press.

3. *Legal Pleadings*: Allegations in pleadings should not be reported as more than simple allegations. Judicial officers and the press should be mindful of injustice or prejudice that may result from pretrial publication of such matters.

4. *Files*: Official files in civil actions and probate matters, including pleadings, court orders and published depositions, are official records and available to the news media.

5. *Depositions and Interrogatories*: Until opened and filed by court rule or order, a deposition is not an official document, not a part of the clerk's file in the cause and not available to the news media. After court publication it may be extracted, quoted or copied for public dissemination except any portions which may have been stricken.

Reporting prior to trial what was said in a deposition may prejudice prospective jurors. Premature reporting may be unfair if, on the reading of the deposition in open court, portions are stricken.

Answers to written interrogatories, filed with the clerk, are as much a part of the public record as are depositions which have been opened and filed.

News reports should reflect whether the statements in depositions or answers to interrogatories have been uttered in open court or only in a filed document.

6. *Confidential Proceedings*: Adoption, mental illness and family court causes, are by their nature and by statute, entitled to special protection by the court. Investigative reports are generally confidential. In those cases where the news media desire access to such records or hearings, application may be made to the discretion of the court.

7. *Estates and Guardianships*: The probate of estates of decedents and the administration of guardianships are usually non-adversary proceedings, conducted in open court without verbatim reporting by an official reporter. Newsmen should have access to all such hearings, to the official files concerning them and to such information as can be supplied by counsel and court attaches. Because of the nature of estate matters, personal and financial data concerning the decedent and his family must be revealed to the court. Whether it should be given to the public by the news media should be governed by good taste, and the public's need to know, balanced against the potential effects on the survivors.

8. *Summary Dispositions*: Disposition of civil actions by summary judgment or dismissal is a judicial determination which may appropriately be reported. The news media should be encouraged to report the reasons for the court's action. The court should make these reasons available.

9. *Fair Trial*: Litigants in civil causes, including causes having special news value because of public interest in the subject matter, are as much entitled to a fair trial by an unbiased jury as is a criminal defendant. Jurors summoned to decide questions of civil liability or damages should be free from public clamor and special influences. News media should be wary of contrived information, the effect of which would be to influence potential jurors as to liability or amount of damage awards. The media acknowledge that the pretrial reporting of civil cases may involve the same risks to the administration of justice as the pretrial reporting of criminal cases. Pretrial coverage of civil cases should be balanced to minimize this risk.

Newsmen should use care in reporting portions of jury trials which take place in the temporary absence of the jury. To publicize the court's rulings as to evidentiary matters, may cause jury prejudice.

10. *Successive Related Cases*: When two or more related civil jury cases are being tried in series, the reporting of one disposition may prejudicially affect subsequent trials. The media should exercise restraint to minimize influence on jurors in such matters.

11. *Public Understanding*: Representatives of the news media should be encouraged to attend the trials and other steps of civil matters to the end that the public may understand the judicial process.

12. *Names of Counsel*: Counsel should not use a court proceeding to advertise his skill. Lawyers present evidence and should seek no plaudits in the public press if courts or juries accept their arguments. It is unethical for a lawyer to seek personal publicity following a jury verdict or court determination.

13. *Incomplete Reporting*: Civil suits have two sides. It is unfair to report only a portion of the facts presented at a trial, as though they were the only facts. Trials proceed without regard to deadline. Reporting of only one aspect of a case to meet a deadline may give the follow up in a subsequent report with the other side of the story. Incomplete reporting of civil trials or reporting only those cases on which the newsman has had a helpful tip can give a distorted picture of courthouse news.

14. *Personal Opinions of Counsel*: The Canons of Professional Ethics forbid a lawyer from arguing to the court or jury his personal belief in his client's innocence or in the justice of his cause. He should also refrain from similar statements to the press.

15. *Judge As a News Source*: Because the trial judge has notes of the trial, he may be the best source of verification of evidence introduced in open court, other than the official court reporter. In the absence of other sources available to the newsman, he may ask the judge for verification of facts, but not for comment on the merits of the case prior to judgment or verdict. The judge should avoid any public statement which might prejudice rights on appeal.

16. *Mutual Confidence*: Judges should show appropriate courtesy to newsmen assigned to courthouse beats. They should recognize that newspapers and broadcasters have deadlines and that newsmen must complete their daily assignments within those prescribed times. There should be mutual confidence between the two. The judge may supply background information with the understanding that he will not be quoted and that the information will not be misused. The newsman is under no obligation to withhold publicity of judicial comments made to third persons.

GUIDELINES ON PUBLIC RECORDS

1. Free access to public records is of paramount importance if the public is to be fully informed, and the bench, bar and press have an equal interest in and responsibility to see that this access is maintained.

2. Except where confidentiality is specifically provided for in

statutes, all records which must be maintained by law are clearly open to the public.

3. Every effort should be made to educate not only those among the bar, bench and press but other public officials as well as to the statutes, Supreme Court decisions, attorney general opinions and other authorities bearing on the subject of public records.

4. Any effort by an individual or group to suppress or conceal a public record should be resisted and exposed by the Bench, Bar and Press.

5. The subcommittee should work toward persuading all persons involved to transcribe public records as quickly as possible and make them available to the public.

6. In cases involving matters of public interest, it is entirely proper for the judge writing the opinion or decision to summarize his holding in a paragraph or two to aid the news media in properly interpreting the decision to the public. This is especially important in cases where the opinion is technical or involved.

7. Members of the Bench and Bar should make every effort to be available to answer questions by communications media representatives regarding public records, and representatives of the media should be sufficiently trained to properly interpret legal actions.

8. The committee urges that public records by arresting officers, whether state, county or city, be kept in numbered sequence.